# MONESSEN
## A TYPICAL STEEL COUNTRY TOWN

*Workers appear to be mopping up the construction of one of Monessen's finest buildings, the Monessen Savings and Trust Company building at the corner of Fifth Street and Donner Avenue. It stands today. (Monessen Public Library and District Center.)*

THE
# MAKING OF AMERICA
SERIES

# MONESSEN
## A TYPICAL STEEL COUNTRY TOWN

## CASSANDRA VIVIAN

ARCADIA
PUBLISHING

Published by Arcadia Publishing
Charleston SC, Chicago IL, Portsmouth NH, San Francisco CA

Printed in the United States

Library of Congress control number: 2002104297

For all general information contact Arcadia Publishing at:
Telephone 843-853-2070
Fax 843-853-0044
E-Mail sales@arcadiapublishing.com
For customer service and orders:
Toll-Free 1-888-313-2665

Visit us on the Internet at www.arcadiapublishing.com

*The Monessen Fire Department still has its 1915 Chemical truck, its 1942 Seagrave serial truck, and this 1923 Seagrave pumper. Only seven of the pumpers were made; only two are running: this one and one in a musuem. (Greater Monessen Historical Society.)*

# CONTENTS

Acknowledgments 6

1. In the Beginning . . . 8

2. The New Klondike 17

3. War, Pestilence, and Denial: A Decade of Terror 40

4. Living Life in America 61

5. Finding Power, Rejecting Republicanism 79

6. Scandal, War, and More Scandal 93

7. As Good as It's Gonna Get 106

8. Poor Choices, Bad Decisions 122

9. The Long Slide 134

10. Is There a Future for Monessen? 147

Bibliography 157
Index 159

# ACKNOWLEDGMENTS

This book about the history of my hometown is dedicated to my grandparents, Peter Vivian (Pietro Viviani) and Ida Cavalli Vivian (Viviani), who were in Monessen by 1900, and Nazzareno Parigi and Santa Carolina Paggini Parigi, who were here by 1913.

They lived this story. Through them, this book is dedicated to all the immigrant men and women who gave up lives in other lands and sailed the ocean to an unknown place and a new life with fear in the pit of their stomachs, but courage in their hearts. Monessen and towns like it all over the United States are their legacy.

My thanks go to the following:

Mitch Steen is the "Father" of Monessen history. He wrote a longtime column in the *Daily,* and eventually the *Valley Independent.* Anyone who looks at the history of the Mon Valley must begin with Mitch and build upon his firm foundation. His collection of materials, left in several libraries in the Mon Valley, repeat his many newspaper columns and is a tribute to his love of this valley.

The *Valley Independent* and other valley newspapers have created an invaluable record of life in Monessen: its news, its prejudices, its joys, its sorrows, and its pride. No book on the community can be written without consulting them again and again.

Monessen is fortunate to have the Monessen Public Library and District Center and the good people who work there. They have assisted me many times without question.

To the readers who helped check facts and voice opinions on this complicated topic: Jack Bergstein, Jean Delare Davies, Pete Demas, Richard L. George, IdaBelle Minnie, Raymond Johnson II, Anthony Mascetta, Nick Stafferi, Susanna Swade, Chuck Zubritsky, and Danny Zyglowicz.

To the people and organizations that provided photographs and/or information: Stephanie Milinovich Buchar, Vincentine Cecelia, Robert Cook, Anna Crump, David J. Dyky, George Essey, Helen Olsavick Ezerski, Frederick Feldman, Regina Feryak, Alvin Frick, Greater Monessen Historical Society, Elizabeth "Betty" Meyer Frick, Clifford Jones, Lee and Lois Jones, Deanna Zborowski Kreger, Emma Jene Lelik, George Loukas, Ed Mikula, Reno and Rena Moncini,

Monessen Public Library and District Center, Monessen Redevelopment Authority, Eli Myer, Ralph Palmer, Jay N. Polkabla, Nancy Revak, Peter "Bud" Roman, Daniel "Boots" Salotti, Ruth Stern Schrag, Teresa Sinchak, David Victoria, and Joan Zubritsky.

A special thanks to Ruth Victoria and her staff at Victoria House, who assisted in caring for my mom while I ran around talking, photographing, and sitting in front of a microfilm machine at the library.

An apology for all the historic events that happened in Monessen that are not recorded here. Another apology for the sometimes-simplistic approach to rather complicated issues that appear here. These omissions are due to a lack of space, not a lack of desire to investigate further. I have tried to present the history of the people and their city, while, at the same time, being kind to those who lived it or are living it today. Although we can claim the glory for the good deeds of our ancestors, we are not responsible for their misdeeds. All facts in this book are documented.

*The author's grandmother Carolina Parigi (far left), grandfather Nazzareno Parigi (far right), and mother Elizabeth (third from right with tie) enjoy a chicken roast on a farm in Star Junction. The spit is a Pittsburgh Steel "government job," a personal job made on company time with company materials.*

# 1. In the Beginning . . .

Monessen didn't just happen. When the big bang stopped shaking up the universe at the dawn of time, that was the beginning of Monessen. Millions of years and a lot of additional shakeups would slide Monessen into its present location. Collisions, compressions, fire, and brimstone would combine the right ingredients to make the spot perfect for an industrial community.

When land masses collided to form the single continent of Gondwana back in the Precambrian Era (900 million years ago), the African continent collided with North America and then drifted away. The encounter created folding and creasing as easily as crushing a piece of tin foil. In the Ordovician Period (500 million years ago), the continents crept together again until they collided to form the super-continent of Pangaea, resulting in more creases and folds. Finally, the two continents whacked for a third time. The accordion-like ripples North America sustained by such impacts created the ridges and peaks of what we call the Appalachian system, with the Allegheny Mountains at their heart. That accounts for the ridges and valleys of Pennsylvania's Appalachian Plateau, a plateau that nestles Monessen in one of its valleys.

While most of this upheaval was occurring, Monessen was well below the equator. In fact, it was near the south pole and had been subjected to incredible winds and extreme temperatures. Its evolution continued. A great deal of the time, Monessen was under water in a shallow marine environment. Digging in Monessen may unearth a sea fossil or two. Heading for Route 906 and looking at the limestone ridges should reveal fossils there as well. All of these remnants are the gifts of the ancient seas. One more piece of the earth's groundwork for Monessen was in place.

Perhaps the most important ingredient for the creation of Monessen was laid down in the Pennsylvanian time (280 to 320 million years ago) of the Carboniferous Period of the Paleozoic Era. That third continent collision pushed Monessen up out of the water. The atmosphere turned warm and wet as Pennsylvania moved north and close to the equator. Trees started to grow, big ferns followed, and little insects and animals like amphibians, dragonflies, and cockroaches began skittering about. Through the growth, death, and rebirth of the plants and animals, much carbon was formed. Once the carbon was submerged in its own bulk and denied oxygen, it became peat. Over time, new layers of sand and silt covered the peat and pressurized it until it sizzled into coal. More and more coal formed; in fact, the area gradually became the site of one of the world's greatest deposits of the substance. Today, these deposits are called the great Pittsburgh Coal Seam, the basis for the impressive coal and steel industry in southwestern Pennsylvania. This is the reason Monessen was founded on this land.

In what we call the Glacier Age, huge ice flows began to move south to the edges of Pennsylvania. The first was the Wisconsin Glacier, which began about 18,000 years ago and lasted for nearly 8,000 years, reaching as far south as Moraine State Park near Butler. In fact, the name "Moraine" means stone debris deposited by a glacier. The 1-mile-deep sheet of ice created valleys, streams, rivers, and lakes wherever it went, changing the landscape and affecting the rivers in the Monessen area. The most important change was the creation of Lake Monongahela.

Lake Monongahela flooded most of future Monessen. The current Monongahela River is 710 feet above sea level at the water's edge, but the lake was 1,060 feet above sea level. That means that only the portions of the community higher than Parkway and McKee Avenues were above the waters of the ancient lake: no downtown, no hollows, no Park Plan. Lake Monongahela did one other thing to

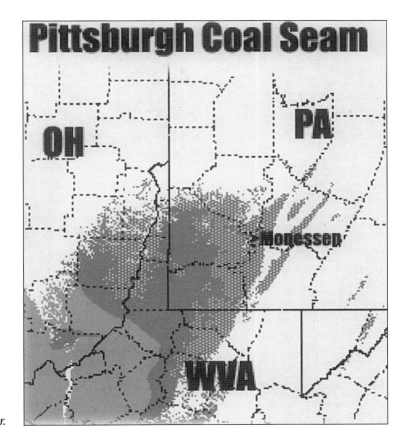

*The Pittsburgh Coal Seam extends through several modern states and includes Monessen, which is in Westmoreland County along the Monongahela River.*

*Here is a primeval view of the Monongahela River at Monessen prior to locks, dams, and industrialization. This is how it must have appeared to early inhabitants. (Ed Mikula.)*

prime the site of Monessen. Prior to the glacier, all of the river systems flowed north independently and emptied into Lake Erie. When Lake Monongahela drained for the last time, the Allegheny and Ohio Rivers changed their courses and began to flow south. The Monongahela continued to flow north, but it met up with the other two rivers at the Point in modern Pittsburgh to form a system that is part of the drainage of a major portion of North America. This made any town along these rivers strategically important. The land was ready.

We simply do not know who was here first. One of the oldest sites in southwestern Pennsylvania is the Meadowcroft Rock Shelter, which shows evidence of possible habitation as many as 20,000 years ago. Were any of those people ever in Monessen's bend of the river? The evidence shows that they moved around a lot, hunting for animals like caribou, mastodon, and mammoth. We do know a little more about the next group of people, the Mound Builders. They were not one, but at least three and probably more, distinct peoples: the Hopewell culture from the mid-west, the Mississippian culture from the south, and the Adena culture from Ohio, West Virginia, New York, and Pennsylvania.

The Adena people lived between 1000 B.C. and 700 A.D. in the Woodland Period. They were a highly developed culture not only of hunters and gatherers, but of farmers and builders. They learned to use the land and the river to their best advantage. They farmed seeded vegetables like barley, allowing them to settle down and establish villages. The most interesting evidence of their culture are the mounds of earth they constructed for burial and ceremonial purposes. None of these constructions are known to be in Monessen, but one exists in Rostraver Township on what was once Shepler's Farm. Unquestionably, the Adena killed a deer, a bear, or a squirrel on Monessen land, or laid a few traps in the river for fish.

The next known inhabitants of the land are called the Monongahela People. Not much is known about them either, even though 400 sites attributed to them have been discovered along the Monongahela, Youghiogheny, and Casselman Rivers. They lived in small stockaded villages of between 100 and 150 families and farmed vegetables like squash, maize, and even beans. The Monongahelians died out just as William Penn was receiving his land grant from the King of England in 1681, perhaps from the new diseases brought to the American shores by the invading Europeans, or perhaps by merely integrating with the new influx of Native Americans in the area.

Once the Monongahelians were gone, other tribes appeared. Their names can be found all over western Pennsylvania: Shawnee State Park, Mingo Creek, Seneca Street, Delaware Avenue, even the Monongahela River carries a Native American name. "Monongahela" is Delaware for "river with falling in banks," signifying one of the main land features of southwestern Pennsylvania: landslides. Every spring, some hillside slips and falls and some property owner is devastated. The Delaware were an Eastern Pennsylvania tribe that had been pushed further and further west into Monessen's territory and, eventually, beyond.

The *Short History of Westmoreland County* reports that there were several Native American villages in Monessen's vicinity. There were 30 known sites between Brownsville and Pittsburgh alone. In the first quarter of the twentieth century, a man named George Fisher went looking for these sites. He found one on the McMahon family property, which makes it a true Monessen site. Fisher called it site #30, but it appears to have been lost in time. When the Monessen Brewery was being destroyed in the early 1940s, a small village was unearthed there, too, which could be a second site. On Shepler's Hill, just outside Monessen, four separate villages once existed overlooking the river.

Even when settlers finally began to fill the spaces around the Monongahela River, they ignored the bend in the river that would eventually be Monessen. Yet, almost every great event that took place in western Pennsylvania's colonial past required marching through or sailing by Monessen. Traders like George Groghan, Christopher Gist, Thomas Cresap, and William Trent came to the Monongahela between 1748 and 1750 for the Ohio Company. They settled elsewhere, but perhaps set some of their traps here, since they clearly passed by. Mike Fink, the great keel boater, had to pass future Monessen on his travels on the three rivers. The French and Indian War happened all around Monessen from Brownsville to the south to Pittsburgh to the north.

The flatlands may have been swampy, but the hills surrounding the river bend had great farming potential. One by one, farmers began buying up property. The families of Manown, McMahon, Luce, and Owens owned acreage. Soon, they discovered that the soil was perfect for growing rye, and, because of the taxes placed on shipping farm goods back east to market, it was better to convert the bulky rye into whiskey, which took up less space. Every farm had a still, every still made good ol' Monongahela Rye, and every pack horse headed east or west was loaded down with whiskey. The soil gave the brew a special flavor and the whiskey was in demand throughout the colonies.

Beating the system didn't last long. Alexander Hamilton, secretary of the treasury, needed a way to pay for the Revolutionary War, and he soon noticed all the free whiskey making its way east and west from the Monongahela Valley. Many area farmers had won this land as payment for their service in the Revolution. He hit the farmers with a whiskey tax and the Whiskey Rebellion was born. It was the first testing of the fledgling United States Constitution, as well as the country's first rebellion. It was, most importantly, the first time the character of the people of the Monongahela Valley made an impression on the country.

In the end, the stills were broken up and it looked as if the farmers would have to find a new market for their special rye. Nevertheless, legitimate distilleries began cropping up all along the Mon Valley: the Sam Thompson Distillery in Brownsville; the Abraham Overholt and Company Distillery in West Overton; and the largest and best, the John Gibson and Sons Distillery in Gibsonton, near the modern Belle Vernon Bridge over the "Mon" (as the Monongahela River is affectionately called). The Monessen Distilling Company, otherwise known as the Firestone Distilling Company, would come later. Gibson knew whiskey. The Irishman had been making it in Philadelphia for over 20 years and, in 1856, he purchased over 40 acres to build a distillery on the east bank of the Monongahela River. An industry began.

At last, almost everything was in place for this land to bear fruit. Just two more measures were necessary: the establishment of the Pittsburgh Freight Zone and the lifting of the tariff on tin. Monessen's strip of land fell barely within the Pittsburgh Freight Zone, which is more rewarding than one can imagine. Monessen was close enough to Pittsburgh to receive the same special pricing as the Pittsburgh mills. Those Pittsburgh mills devised a pricing system that enabled them to ship their steel around the country at prices competitive with mills closer to the destination of their goods, and Monessen mills, because they were within the freight zone, could do the same.

At around the same time, the federal government passed the McKinley Tariff Act. Up to that time, it was forbidden to manufacture tin in the United States, but with the passage of this act in 1890, tin became a viable business. Speculators came and founded Monessen, but they did not do it for love of the land; they did it to make money, and money they made. Monessen was one of a dozen or more towns that were created at the turn of the century by entrepreneurs from Pittsburgh looking for investments. These communities all followed the same pattern: they boomed at a surprising rate, they leveled off when their industry was at its peak, and they fell into a long decline as their commerce crashed and burned. In a nutshell, that is the story of Monessen.

*The community of McMahon, established by the McMahon family, was a separate colony from Monessen. It was located between Sixth and Tenth Streets above McMahon.*

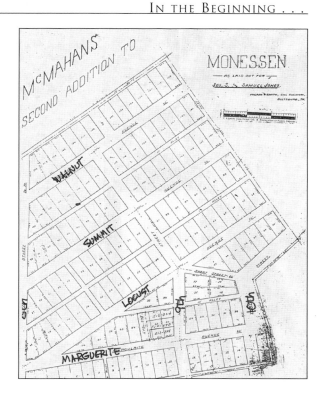

When speculators first came looking in the mid-Mon Valley, there were a number of property owners: William J. Manown, Alexander and Thomas McMahon, Hiram Myers, William Davis, William Cowlishaw, J.H. Somers, Eliza McMahon Smith, and Edward M. Ody. Hugh McMahon had two sons: Alexander, to whom he gave 100 acres in 1873, and Thomas, who, in 1877, received 111 acres along the river from future First Street to Twelfth Street and west, up the hills of Monessen, to current McMahon Avenue.

In 1885, a woman named Margaret Nelson took out a $5,000 mortgage on part of the McMahon land. The Hamilton Company, land speculators, purchased the McMahon land in 1892. They wanted to found a community called Fordham after Lock Number 4 and its dam on the Mon. They went so far as to create a plan, which they had recorded at the county offices in 1893. However, they never paid the Nelson mortgage. The land went into foreclosure and all 211 acres were purchased by Charles Orr for $23,000. Orr then gave the property to the East Side Land Company. East Side was but one of dozens of companies established to buy and sell land in southwestern Pennsylvania. This particular company was organized in Pittsburgh by Colonel James M. Schoonmaker, Philander C. Knox, James H. Reed, H. Sellers McKee, George O. Morgan, and George B. Motheral. These particular names also constitute the principal avenues of the original town.

The controlling interest in the East Side Land Company belonged to Colonel James M. Schoonmaker, a Pittsburgher who had made a fortune in coal in Fayette

13

County. He owned a number of coke ovens in Dawson, was chairman of Redstone and Morewood Coke Companies, and was vice president of the Pittsburgh and Lake Erie Railroad, the P&LE. Monessen was a win-win investment for him. It guaranteed him a close market for his Fayette County coke, plus trade and travel for his railroad, which he brought through the valley. He made a fortune in the town, investing in such ventures as the First National Bank and the Monessen Water Company, but he never lived there.

William H. Donner did live in Monessen, at least for a short time. He built a home at 435 McKee. Donner got the deal of a lifetime when the speculators offered him 20 acres of prime riverfront land to build a tin mill and $10,000 to help with his relocation. Since his enterprises in Indiana were running out of natural gas and he needed a good fuel source for his mills, Donner took the deal. His mill was the linchpin around which other industries would grow. A few years later, he also founded the Union Steel Company with Henry Clay Frick and two Mellon brothers. That mill gave birth to the town of Donora a few miles north of Monessen ("Do" for Donner and "Nora" for Nora Mellon). Donner was also president of Cambria Steel in Johnstown, the Pennsylvania Steel Company, and the Donner Steel Company in Buffalo, New York. When his son died of cancer at a young age, in 1932, Donner turned his focus and his money to cancer research.

*William Donner was the founder of the National Tin Plate Company in Monessen. The company soon became the National Works of the American Sheet and Tin Plate Company of United States Steel. In Monessen, it was always called the Tin Mill.*

Philander C. Knox was a Brownsville man. Later in life, he became a senator, then secretary of state, and, finally, the attorney general of the United States. Judge James H. Reed, Knox's law partner, was a corporate lawyer by profession and lived in Allegheny (North Side), becoming a judge in 1891. He had to give up the position because of ill health. H. Sellers McKee, who lived in Allegheny as well, was into natural gas and glass. He and his brothers formed McKee and Brothers. When a large pocket of natural gas was found at Grapeville, along Route 30, he speculated on a new nearby community and named it Jeannette. Monessen and Jeannette, one glass and one tin and steel, were both successes for McKee. In addition to being a founder, George B. Motheral and four other men took out a charter for the Monessen Steel Company at $500 a share, but, although there was an Independent Steel Company on the Sandborn Map of 1908, Motheral's mill doesn't seem to have gone very far.

These men turned over the running of their venture to the company they created: the East Side Land Company. It was M.J. Alexander, the general manager of the company, who gave the community its name: "Mon" for the river and "essen" for Essen, Germany, the great steel capital where the mills of Krupp were located. These German mills would be the driving engines for supplying munitions to the German army during World War I and World War II, while its sister city along the Mon in Pennsylvania was part of the great "Arsenal for Democracy" that did the same for the American and Allied armies.

Throughout its tenure in Monessen, the East Side Land Company, which closed in 1922, was run by a very interesting personality named H. Dallas McCabe. McCabe was not only a stockholder of the company, but he sat on the board of directors and served as its general manager. McCabe was a surveyor and created the look of the community when he laid out the lots for East Side. His influence was everywhere. He was a director of the Webster, Monessen, Belle Vernon, and Fayette City Street Railway Company, the Monessen Savings and Trust Company, the First National Bank of Monessen, and the Monessen Foundry and Machine Company. He was also superintendent of the Monessen Water Company, which opened in 1901.

Two other land companies completed the riverfront look of Monessen. Manown developed East Monessen, while West Monessen became a Standard Land and Improvement Company undertaking. In 1901, Samuel Jones of Belle Vernon bought 20 acres, which he divided into plots of land. He named the new area "McMahon." By 1910, McMahon had become an independent borough with 813 residents. On February 24, 1912, it was incorporated into Monessen. Following McMahon came the Essen Land Company, which purchased 40 acres of land in 1905. Jones asked George Nash and C.F. Eggers to join him. One can almost guess the location of this venture, since Monessen has a Jones Street and a Nash Street.

Next came the Monessen Improvement Company, founded around 1902 by G.F. Wright, E.B. Sloterbeck, Eli H. Wolf, W.P. Kirk, Jesse Hancock, and R.E. Palmer, all local businessmen. Over the next few years, they built and financed about 100 homes. Part of that development was on Knox between Sixth and Ninth. When the new Junior and Senior High Schools were built at the corners of Sixth, Reed, and Knox, the houses on that property were moved to vacant lots in the area. The company then began building homes on Graham, McKee, Braddock, Clarendon, and Aliquippa. In 1925, they built an additional 20 homes on Graham Avenue (originally part of the McMahon estate), said to be the most modern in the city. Ralph E. Palmer III, a longtime dentist in Monessen, recalls that during the Depression, the partner responsible for the cash kept too much for himself and ended up in jail.

On July 27, 1897, the first Sale Day took place and the first plot of land was sold. It was a muddy mess, for much was swampland, leading to the nickname "Mud-essen." Streets and lots were marked off by pegs and string, and not much level land could be bought. Squatters had set up homesteads in wagons or tents on the land they hoped to buy. Samuel Jones was the first man to purchase land for his Monessen Lumber Company at Ninth Street and Donner. When the gavel came down on the sale of that property, Monessen was in business.

*An East Side Land Company ad, which appeared in the* Monessen News *special issue called "Monessen Illustrated 1902" not only promotes buying land but owning homes.*

# 2. THE NEW KLONDIKE

Monessen exploded. Shovel by shovel, the billion-year-old earth flew everywhere as buildings began rising from McCabe's carefully laid-out plat. Industry was going up along the river, commercial buildings along newly named Schoonmaker and Donner Avenues, and hotels, boarding houses, and family residences along the hollows and hillsides in a frenzy of activity. Monessen was defining itself.

The din of the construction must have been heard in Pittsburgh. Workers dug with picks and shovels, horses' hooves clopped, and wagon wheels whizzed, hauling materials on muddy streets. Labor gangs stacked block on streets for the steady hands of bricklayers. Lumber companies like Peoples, Motz, and Westmoreland provided supplies and built the community building by building. As there were no true roads, the P&LE railway station and freight house were among the busiest places in town. The railroad and the river were the best way in and out of Monessen. The quiet ripples of the river along the bend would be heard no more. For better or worse, wilderness was morphing into an industrial revolution.

In May 1897, a year before the official founding of Monessen, construction for Donner's tin mill began. It rose along the river, smack in the center of the new town, beyond Fifth Street and Donner (now Kopper's coke ovens). Its smokestacks bellowed smoke over the town for decades. No sooner was it operating than it was sold and its name changed to the American Sheet and Tin Plate Company. By 1904, it had 25 separate mills and was, according to the *History of Westmoreland County*, "one of the largest and most thoroughly equipped tin plate plants in the world." The very first phone in Monessen, installed in 1898, belonged to this mill. Its neighbor, the Monessen Box Company, produced boxes for shipping the tin. At its peak, the box company made 4,000 boxes a day and employed 35 men. By 1919, the Tin Mill employed 1,600 men and women.

As the Tin Mill was rising in the middle of town, W.S. Bumbaugh of McKeesport lifted a shovelful of dirt on June 21, 1898 to produce iron and brass casting in the Monessen Foundry at Donner Avenue and Thirteenth Street. It stood where the offices and blooming mill of Pittsburgh Steel would eventually rise. It moved, dramatically, over the weekend of September 23, 1902 (not 1918 as is often quoted). Since Pittsburgh Steel wanted to locate to the same area, and

*J. Wallace Page, the founder of Page Woven Wire and Fence Company, never lived in Monessen. The main office for the mill would eventually be located in the Frick building in Pittsburgh. (Greater Monessen Historical Society.)*

the foundry needed more space, Monessen Foundry moved to 4 acres on the east end of Donner at Manown near the Monessen Brewery. In one of historian Mitch Steen's many newspaper columns, he describes the move:

> After the week's work had been completed Saturday night, a crew of men was set to work at dismantling the plant and loading it onto freight cars . . . 40 cars of machinery had been loaded with three 25-ton cranes, 3,000 different patterns for casting and 500 flacks making up some of the variety of equipment, which was moved . . . the same crew went to work putting it together again. Monday morning, within 24 hours of the time the dismantling began, the factory was ready for operation in its new location.

In 1931, the foundry beat out 20 bidders to make the valve operating machinery for Lock Number 4 along the river nearby. In 1945, the foundry would be sold to Rockwell Manufacturing Company and instead of making Golden Anderson Valves and Pittsburgh Valves for water companies, it began to make gas meters and parking meters for the entire country. Chances are that most of the gas meters in homes in Monessen came from the foundry. The town parking meters definitely did not, but that story will come later.

The American Steel Hoops Company was the next mill to rise (1899) on Monessen soil. The factory produced barrel hoops for the kegs that carried materials like nails. First, however, the riverfront had to be adjusted. The hoops company was on riverfront swamp, formerly part of David Owens's farm. To level the hilly land, a 20- to 30-foot layer of slag was laid, then leveled off to produce a high cliff at the water's edge. Once the mill was up and running, additional debris from the mill, including bad ingots, iron, and even steel, was used to create a seawall. It didn't always stop the river from flooding the mills and the town, but when the Monongahela got violent, Monessen fared better than most.

In 1900, the founders hooked another big business. J. Wallace Page of Rollin, Michigan, who also operated a mill in Adrian, Michigan, bought a 22-acre riverfront plot of land from the Manown Farm. The Page Woven Wire and Fence Company was constructed where First Street intersected Donner. Part of that facility is still standing. Page invented the woven wire fence and employed 500 men to produce 3,000 tons of it a month at the Monessen facility. Page built the fence from scratch and had his own blooming mill, open hearth, rod mill, and wire mill. In 1920, the facility was sold to the American Chain Company.

While Page was beginning operations, Wallace J. Rowe, formerly of U.S. Steel, was creating the Pittsburgh Steel Company. Rowe purchased 60 acres of riverfront property, bought out the hoops company, and began building various mills. Pittsburgh Steel, the company that would allow the community to thrive for the next 70 years, was born. The company was erected so fast that it was hard to keep track of just what was happening. Rowe built the rolling mills, followed

*The main office and factory of Page Woven Wire and Fence Company, c. 1911, was just across the railroad tracks beyond Second and Donner. Today, a guardhouse stands at that location. (Greater Monessen Historical Society.)*

*Workers raised the building over the foundations of the newly constructed open hearth furnaces at Pittsburgh Steel in 1907. The photographer, Datz, had an established business in Monessen and took many of the early city images, both industrial and mercantile. (Ed Mikula.)*

by the galvanizing department, which, in July 1902, was the first department of the mill to begin operations. In August, three more departments—fence, barbed wire, and staple—opened for business.

In September, the Number 1 Rod Mill began producing 400 tons of nails a day with 3,000 employees working two 12-hour shifts at 20¢ an hour. The din, added to the sounds of the growing town, must have been loud enough to scare away all the cats from Wild Cat Hollow. One thing was sure; most of Monessen never spent a penny on a nail. They "borrowed" a few from the nail mill. Every house in town was surely pounded into place with Pittsburgh Steel nails, which were sold all over the country. We know from the reports of the trial that Bruno Hauptmann, the accused murderer of the Lindbergh baby, used Pittsburgh Steel nails to construct the ladder he built. The prosecution was trying to determine when the nails were purchased, but could not, "as this brand of nails is shipped to practically all jobbers and dealers throughout the United States."

Pittsburgh Steel was unstoppable in its vision. The company bought Monessen Coal and Coke and the Seamless Tubing Company of America, which was built in 1904. Instead of using the less controlled Bessemer converter to make steel, the company broke ground with eight 95-ton, open hearth furnaces on March

13, 1907. This innovation would put the new facility at the cutting edge of steel manufacturing when it went into production on August 4, 1908.

At the end of the decade, Pittsburgh Steel was still building and growing. The company was trying to create a totally independent operation, solely reliant on its own materials and production. It would battle its entire life to keep its mills integrated, keep raw materials close at hand, have its own steel to feed its finishing sides, and keep the plants modernized. The latter was an almost impossible task for such a huge factory, but to the end in the 1980s, that is what it did.

Aside from these larger industries, there were also a bevy of smaller works: Monessen Brick Works; Eggers and Graham, manufacturers of building materials; Monessen Mattress and Bedding Company; Monongahela Valley Electric Company (1899); Monessen Distilling Company; Monessen, Belle Vernon, Fayette City Street Railway Company (1903); Monessen General Hospital (1909); and even the Monessen skating rink.

Three newspapers had opened in Monessen by 1902. The first was the weekly *Monessen News*, founded by Charles E. Federman, which opened in 1899. By 1902, it was operated by feisty C.L. Schuck. The second was the *Monessen Leader,* whose founder was the sheriff of Westmoreland County, John H. Tresher, and whose managing editor was Joseph R. Bailey. It came out weekly. The last newspaper was the *Daily Independent*, founded by F. Householder. Harry Pore was managing editor by 1902. Later, the *Monessen Call* would be founded, more a magazine than a newspaper. They were all Republican-oriented publications. The only paper operating today is the *Independent* and it is now called the *Valley Independent*. These newspapers chronicled the day-to-day lives of the industries and people of Monessen. They present the drama of life, the justice and injustice, the scheming, and the glory of Monessen.

The busiest office in town was the East Side Land Company, the owner of Monessen, but to get to it, you had to walk over a boardwalk that bridged the thick mud. Donner Avenue, like the mills, had another problem: it was on the floodplain. It flooded at least once or twice in a 100-year period. Each building on Donner was and is required to have a pump installed in its basement to pump the floodwater out. Sometimes, the boards of the boardwalk did not match the entrance to a business and there was a bit of juggling by customers to get from one to the other. Regardless of the inconvenience, it was a buyer's market in Monessen.

By 1903, lots were selling for between $250 and $350, with no interest, no taxes, deferred payments if the person became ill, and money refunded if the buyer died. Anyone would buy under these terms. Even before the businesses began to open, the fledgling community of Monessen became a borough. This encouraged merchants from all over western Pennsylvania to invest in Monessen. Many did not move to the noisy, mostly foreign place, but they did open stores. The first storeroom to go up was occupied by Meyer and Son, a clothier that opened on Donner Avenue in 1899. Some even erected their own buildings. By 1904, the town had grown enough that four girls graduated from the high school.

A man named William A. McShaffrey speculated that Monessen would support a performance center. He opened the Monessen Opera House at Fifth Street and Schoonmaker on December 4, 1904 with a production of *Captain Barrington*. Anton Fritz, who also built several other projects in the city, built the opera house of brick. Tickets cost 25¢, 35¢, and 75¢, but the venue never truly made money. By 1920, after it had been vacant for many years, the Opera House was sold to the Slovak Independent Political Organization. Eventually, it burned down.

McShaffrey moved to Monessen and joined the Masons, the Elks, the Eagles, and the Monessen Board of Trade. Soon, he began speculating in the valley. He opened the Dreamland Theatre of Monongahela, another in Charleroi, and a fourth in Donora. He was a theater man, having appeared "on the boards" himself in productions in Pittsburgh. McShaffrey was also a stockholder and director of the valley's only trolley park, the Eldora Amusement Park across the river in Washington County. Then, he opened what would become a longtime landmark in the community: the Star Theater.

Monessen was showing promising signs of growth. The town had a police force, a fire brigade, a burgess, and a ruling body. It had churches, schools, houses, hotels, newspapers, banks, telephones, a water company, a railroad depot, street cars, grocers, candy shops, harness shops, stables, lumber yards, barbershops, an opera house, a few gambling dens, and a small, but thriving, red light district. It even had a ferry that crossed the river from the bottom of Ninth Street to the awaiting trains at the base of the mountain on the far shore. (The Monessen Ferry

*The first Monessen Municipal building stood on the corner of Fourth and Donner and contained the fire hall and the jail. People could talk to the prisoners from the sidewalk. Kirk's Drug Store is in the white brick building (still standing) on the right. (Greater Monessen Historical Society.)*

*The Star Theater on Sixth Street was a magnet for pedestrians. Beside it is what may have been the beginnings of Johnson's Restaurant. The family says the restaurant opened with a hot plate, a coffee pot, and a few cups and saucers. (Greater Monessen Historical Society.)*

Company had to erect wooden steps on the other side so people could climb up from the river to the trains.) With all of this in place, folks began to flock to the community.

The story of Monessen is not only the story of industry or public buildings. Those stories have been told before. People create the personality of Monessen. The town was at the vanguard of a great experiment. At no other time in the history of the modern world were so many people from so many different cultures thrown together in small communities to try to live, work, and become a nation. Monessen's story is this great melting pot. Its struggle to find common ground within the community was the nation's struggle to do the same. It was not an easy road. In addition to various nationalities, the people divided themselves into three basic groups of citizens: the "Americans," the "Foreigners," and the "Coloreds." Each saw the community through a different lens. The friction between groups, the hardships they endured, separately and together, and the discrimination they all felt is the Monessen story. It is this blending that made the citizens eventually become the Americans they all hoped to be. But it wasn't always easy.

Parkway, McKee, and Reed Avenues had the largest and grandest homes in the community with hardwood floors, electric lights, grand oak or mahogany staircases, cut glass doorways, and some indoor plumbing. The best were on "Silk Stocking Row," the homes on McKee Avenue from Fourth through Ninth Streets. These homes definitely were among the 32 subscribers that the new telephone company serviced in 1900. The people who occupied these streets were bosses in the mills and merchants in the community. Their names appeared at the tops of newly erected commercial buildings downtown. They became city officials and employees. They were predominately Scotch, Irish, German, English, and very, very Republican. Above all, they were considered the "Americans," since they had come to America in a much earlier wave of immigration than the African Americans and southern and eastern Europeans. The newspapers addressed themselves to them and called the other Europeans in the community the "aliens," "foreigners," or "undesirables."

These "Americans" had their babies at Dudas's Maternity Hospital on McKee. Their churches were featured prominently on the main streets: First Methodist (1898), Trinity Episcopal, First United Presbyterian (1898), First Christian Church (1900), and the first Catholic church in Monessen, St. Leonard's (1900). They also filled the ranks of the newly formed Elks (1902) and Masons, while the women founded such groups as the Woman's Club of Monessen (1911) and the Evening Woman's Club (1916).

The "Foreigners" were mostly southern and eastern European farmers and workers. They came for a host of different reasons. When the great immigration began, some were "birds of passage," coming to the United States to work for a few years and then returning home. Others left their native land and never looked back, trying to forget even the name of their hometown. Their houses

*Stanley Sinchak stands in front of his grocery store at 321 Schoonmaker Avenue. In 1924, there were 120 such stores in Monessen neighborhoods catering to the tastes of different ethnic groups. (Teresa Sinchak.)*

were mostly large enough to accommodate their big families, plus a few boarders. They often had facilities for bathing, but had outdoor toilets and were without electricity. A few of these outhouses can still be seen in the community, now converted to sheds in backyards. Basements substituted for butcher shops as animals were slaughtered and turned into ethnic specialties like salami, sausages, prosciutto, headcheese, and hams. People made wine, schnapps, and whiskey in their basements as well. A coal furnace provided heat for the residence. Each winter, the coal companies would dump coal in front of houses and someone would have to shovel it into the basement. The house was as warm as the amount of coal burning in the furnace. On cold winter mornings, after the furnace had not been fired all night, houses were freezing and someone would have to go down into the cellar and "fire the furnace." It would take some time to heat up.

The streets in the neighborhoods were dirt, since they would not be paved until the next decade. Backyards were often barnyards. In addition to chickens and rabbits, some folks actually kept cows and pigs. The "Foreign" families kept gardens in the small patches of ground surrounding their residences. They grew things from back home: figs, kohlrabi, zucchini, grapes, garlic, tomatoes, cabbage, and spices like oregano, sage, rosemary, thyme, and cardamom. One of the greatest joys of kids in Monessen in almost every decade was to raid summer gardens on hot steamy nights and sit on street corners, munching freshly picked tomatoes or kohlrabis. The people did more than plant gardens to maintain their ethnicity; they planted language and ideas, too. After school and all over town, Jewish children learned Hebrew, Italian children learned Italian, and Greek children learned Greek. People worked at keeping their heritage alive.

The newly immigrated Germans did not have the status of their cousins the "Americans." The new arrivals lived in Dutchtown, a stretch of land to the east of Second Street, incorporating such streets as Elm, Oak, and Somerset. Of course, they were not Dutch, they were *Deutsche*, the German name for their country and themselves. They built the German Beneficial Union Club (GBU), the first fraternal society in the community, on Second Street and Reed. Many Germans, be they "Foreigners" or "Americans," owned hotels in early Monessen. The Helzelsauer Brothers operated the three-story, 30-room Union Hotel at First Street and Schoonmaker; Fritz, then Baughman, owned the Merchants Hotel on Donner between Fourth and Fifth Streets; Myford operated the Commercial Hotel on Schoonmaker between Second and Third Streets; and Sheetz maintained the Sheetz Hotel in the 1100 block of Schoonmaker. They also maintained businesses. Peter Amman, for example, owned a grocery store at 276 Donner where one could get Limburger cheese and other German delicacies.

The Eastern Europeans were usually labeled with the derogatory terms of "Hunkie" or "Pollock." In fact, they came from a host of tortured and depressed regions: Croatia, Poland, Yugoslavia, Czechoslovakia, the Ukraine, and Russia. They made the same types of foods, but called them by different names. A stuffed cabbage (pig in the blanket) was a *halupki* to a Carpatho-Rusyn woman, who cooked it with tomatoes, but to a Croatian, it was a *sarma* and cooked with sauerkraut, and to a Pole, it was a *galumki*. In all of their clubs, in addition to *halupki*, they feasted on a noodle and cabbage dish called *halushki*; a stuffed dough with cheese, prune, or potato filling called a *pierogi* (*pierohi* to a Ukrainian, *pirohy* to a Slovak); and a stuffed smoked sausage called a *kolbassi*. In later years, so did the rest of the town, who would gladly visit the clubs for a Saturday plate of kraut and kolbassi and a polka or two by a good "Hunkie" band.

By 1901, the first Croatians were in Monessen. Most lived in Wireton, a small community erected by Pittsburgh Steel on riverfront land by what would soon be the Charleroi-Monessen Bridge. They worked mostly in the wire mill and its bundling room at Pittsburgh Steel. It was a habit at the time for a boss to hire from his own ethnic background. After all, many did not speak English and the echoes in the mills flew with the wind in a cacophony of languages. Better to have a Croat give an order to a Croat than have someone get injured. People had to learn other languages, however, a phenomenon that spread in the mills. One African-American boss spoke Croatian, a Slovak learned Italian, while someone else picked up a little Greek.

Wireton was filled with names like Zoretich, Milinovich, and Mihalich. Its streets were Aberdeen, Cass, Bridge, Lewis, Compton, and Aubry. The Croatians divided themselves according to what village they came from. Kids fought each other in the streets of Monessen over ethnic pride thousands of miles away and hundreds of years old. They built two separate clubs for the two factions of Croatians in the community. Both were on Schoonmaker, one near Seventeenth Street, the other near the Charleroi-Monessen Bridge. They could not have been more than 500 steps apart. After 1916, the factions got over their differences and built a single magnificent club, the Croatian Educational and Beneficial Society.

The bakery at Wireton was Filipex and the workers there would try to make all the ethnic pastries "to order," asking each customer how they wanted it. For a Croatian lady, the nut rolls, called *orinacha*, were longer than average, but the Croatians did not eat cold dough cookies at all. In fact, cold doughs, a bite-size version of nut rolls, were probably invented in the United States. That bakery was so successful that its owners built a home on Silk Stocking Row.

During the strike of 1919, Pittsburgh Steel Products Company rearranged Wireton to house strikebreakers. It forced the people out and built barracks for the strikers, actually moving a few homes across the street to get the barracks built. The Croatians moved up to Leeds and Summit and, when the Westgate project of the 1970s tore down most of the buildings from Ninth to Seventeenth Streets, they moved their hall, too. They formed a number of organizations: the Croatian Fraternal Union of America Lodge 191 (May 8, 1902), the Monessen Croatian Social and Educational Society (SLOGA), and the American Croatian Brotherhood.

The Poles, with names like Czelen and Tyberski, came to Monessen in the first waves of immigrants. Many of them were recruited in their home villages, as were other nationalities. Company agents visited small villages with promises of the riches of America and young men would sign up for a new life. In Poland, those agents were often German or Czech. The Monessen Poles lived on Third Street before they began to congregate in "Gory," around Linden Avenue. They erected their club, the Polish National Alliance, on Knox Avenue between Rostraver and Second Street and their church, Saint Hyacinth (1909), on Reed between the same two side streets. Years later, the Polish National Church and the Josef Pilsudski Society, which existed on Third Street, were created. Within Gory was the Famous Bakery run by Casimer Jurkiewcz.

The earliest known Slovak in Monessen was Andy Dudas, who arrived in 1898. Not far behind him were men with familiar Monessen names like Bartus, Bucko, Stofan, Horvat, Kurey, Hromy, Dadas, and Majernik. They lived around Linden, but also at Highland. Many worked in the Tin Mill, the nail mill at Pittsburgh Steel, or at Page's. By 1903, there were enough Slovaks in Monessen to found the Holy Name of Jesus Church on Reed Avenue (1901) and the Slovak Gymnastic Union Sokol. Before the decade was over, there would also be a Slovak Presbyterian Church and, by 1916, a Slovak Home.

All these Slovak organizations had something to do with the multiplicity of their community and their unwillingness to give up their own unique heritage. Where an Italian would have a fig tree in the backyard, a Slovak would have a walnut tree. Nuts were used in everything, but primarily in *kolache*, cookies, like *makovinik orechovnik*, nut and poppy seed rolls. They made their sauerkraut in crocks and eventually shopped for their special items at Troychak, Olsavick, and Chicks Markets in the neighborhoods.

*These newly constructed workmen's houses on East Schoonmaker between First and Second Streets housed mostly Syrians, Russians, and Slavs. During redevelopment in the 1950s and 1960s, the homes were torn down and replaced by Eastgate. Note Page's in the background and the stacks of the Blooming Mill beyond. (Monessen Public Library and District Center.)*

*Saint Mary's Greek Catholic Church was the epicenter for the struggle of Greek Catholic Carpatho-Rusyns to find an identity in the United States. This building no longer stands, having been replaced by a more modern one. (Greater Monessen Historical Society.)*

It is more difficult to define the Carpatho-Rusyns, since they comprise several different groups in Monessen and their road to these divisions was not always an easy one. This complicated story cannot be fully elucidated here, but a simple explanation should provide a general idea.

When the Rusyns came to Monessen, they lacked two things many other immigrants had: a country and an established church in the United States. The closest thing they had to a country was that they came from the Austro-Hungarian Empire. To complicate matters, where labor recruiters would send an entire village of workers from Europe to a single community in the United States (Pricedale's Rusyns came from a village called Losja), Monessen's immigrants came from a number of places because so many workers were needed for the mills. When they arrived in 1898, they settled into two locations: the east end, which became known as Russian Hill, and the west end in a housing complex called Castle Gardens. If they had remained one community in Monessen, they would have been the largest ethnic group in the town. Six thousand Rusyns were recorded in 1920.

The other problem was their religion; they were Greek Catholics. In the eyes of the average person in the United States, they were neither Orthodox nor Catholic, and there was no such religion in the country at the time. By 1902, the Rusyns bought property and built a church, which is still located at Reed and

Second Street, calling it the Dormition of the Mother of God Greek Catholic Church, more commonly known as Saint Mary's. The congregation began the Korjatovych Choir and the Ruska Skola, a Rusyn school for children. The Slovanic Society followed. John Righetti, who compiled this information, tells us the following:

> Wave after wave of challenges hit it [the Rusyn community]. While these challenges fragmented the Rusyn community, they also were the events through which the Monessen Rusyn community became a major player in the history of the Rusyn community in America and Europe.

Simply put, the American Roman Catholic Church wanted the Rusyns to follow their rite, but only if their priests remained celibate and they turned their property over to the Roman bishops. The hard-working Rusyns refused, seeing the suggestion as an infringement on their solitary ownership. Instead, they set up their church as a corporation. Righetti says, "For a disenfranchised group from Europe who never owned or ran anything, in America they owned and ran their own churches—simple immigrants with little education."

The Roman Catholic Church was not about to let them slip away, however. American bishops tried to get the Pope in Rome to force Greek Catholics to join Roman parishes. In 1908, the Pope stated that Greek Catholic clergy in the United States must be celibate and parishes must give up their property to the church. Monessen had one of the largest Greek Catholic communities in the United States and it became the epicenter for this problem. The controversy eventually pushed the congregation in two directions. A portion of the parishioners became the Russian Orthodox and built their own church, Saint John the Divine Russian Orthodox Church. The remainder, wishing to remain Greek Catholic, but still not willing to give up their physical property, had to go to court to keep their identity as Greek Catholics. This division was not an easy one. It split friends and families. It divided brother and sister. It separated father and son. It played itself out on the streets of Monessen. Nonetheless, those who chose to remain Greek Catholics did win their battles in court.

After the split, the Orthodox Rusyns formed the United Russian Orthodox Brotherhood of America (UROBYA). The leader was Peter Ratica and that group is now called Lodge Number 1 of what has become the largest Rusyn Orthodox fraternal organization in the United States. Today, it is called the Orthodox Society of America. None of this information applies completely and totally to every Rusyn, Russian, or Ukrainian family in the community, of course. Each has their unique version.

The majority of the Ukrainians of Monessen are yet another branch of the Rusyns of the Carpathian Mountains in the Austro-Hungarian Empire. They were the third group to break with the Rusyns. This time, it was from the Russian Orthodox, although some had broken from the Greek Catholics years before. Once united, they formed the Ukrainian Literary and Beneficial Association and

Saint Nicholas Ukrainian Church. Their traditions and customs are sprinkled throughout this book.

The Hungarians came from the Austro-Hungarian Empire as well. Originally, there were more Hungarians in Pricedale than there were in Monessen. In fact, Tordy's, the only grocery store catering to Hungarians, was there. It sold kolbassi, *hurka* (a blood pudding), and cured and smoked bacon. Their club, the Hungarian Workingmen's Sick Benefit, Social, and Literary Club, still stands on Parente Boulevard (Seneca). It received its charter in 1904. There is no Hungarian church in Monessen, but many Catholic Hungarians go to Belle Vernon or to one of the other towns with heavy Hungarian settlements, such as Daisytown and Richeyville. One of the biggest celebrations among the Hungarians was a harvest festival called a *Khadas*. After the planting season was over, the Hungarian Hall would be decorated with vines, hanging grapes, and apples, and a festival would be held. They would serve goulash, of course, and maybe chicken paprika with *czeregi*, a twisted flaky fried dough; *pampushkas*, giant doughnuts filled with lekvar; and *palachinta*, crepes with dill and sweet cottage cheese. Then, they would dance the *czardas* and waltz to the music of the violin, a very Hungarian instrument, some of which were made right here in Monessen by a barber on Seneca.

According to the *Keystone Magazine* of Pittsburgh Steel, the first Greek in Monessen was George Katsuleris of Chions (Chios, Thios), Greece. It was not long before others joined him. In fact, the Greek community of Monessen came mostly from fishermen stock on this single Greek island near the Turkish coast. Oral tradition maintains that most of the Greeks in the United States filtered through the mills of Monessen on the way to someplace else. The Greeks lived primarily around Twelfth Street and Schoonmaker and that is where their stores—including the Stupakas Fish Market, later a candy store, at 1260 Schoonmaker; the Harry Croussouloudis restaurant at 1210 Schoonmaker; the Costas Croussouloudis grocery at 1214 Schoonmaker; and Theo Gianodis Dairy at 1116 Schoonmaker—were located. Later, they would expand into Morgan, Parkway, and Highland. In the Tin Mill, Greeks worked as picklers; at Pittsburgh Steel, they were either in the labor gang or wire mill. Sometimes, with their experience as swimmers and divers in the Aegean Sea, Greek workers were asked to dive into the Monongahela and report back on conditions of things underwater. They also operated a number of restaurants like the Victory Restaurant and the Monessen Restaurant.

By 1916, the Greek community founded Saint Spyridon Greek Orthodox Church. This single church once serviced Greek Orthodox families as far away as Uniontown. Through their church, they educated the community on Greek foods, dance, and customs. The folks would feast on *glatoboureko*, a filo square filled with cream; *kourabiethes*, a powdered sugar shortbread with cloves; or the famous *baklava*, filo filled with crushed nuts and honey. In the community, they went into the candy business, opening the Philadelphia Candy Kitchen, the Sugar Bowl, and the Palace of Sweets. They also opened coffeehouses (*Kafeinon*), which were strictly a man's affair with coffee, cards (Greek, of course), backgammon

*Early Italian immigrants pose in front of their first clubhouse on Third Street. Note the typical Italian accordion in the front row and the patriotic waving of the American flag. (Greater Monessen Historical Society.)*

(*tavli*), *ouzo* (a licorice-flavored cordial), newspapers, and talk. Once a year, a puppet show called the *Karagyozy* would come to town and women and children were allowed in the coffeeshop to see the performance.

There were Italians in Monessen as early as 1899. In 1907, an additional 400 to 500 mostly Italian laborers came to Monessen under the auspices of the Gerry Brothers employment agency to build Pittsburgh Steel's open hearth furnaces. They worked mostly in the labor gang and the Number 2 Rod Mill of Pittsburgh Steel. Unlike the Greeks, the Italians came from all over the Italian boot. Like the Rusyns, the Italians were a diversified group identified by region and conquest. The terrain of Italy was diverse, producing different foods, customs, languages, and dresses. It was almost impossible for the various Italian groups to understand each other since Italy had over 1,000 dialects. A Tuscan from the grasslands ate, spoke, and celebrated differently than a Sicilian from the barren, mountainous south. A Neapolitan from the west coast of the peninsula was different from an Abruzzese from the east coast, despite the fact that the two regions met in the middle of the boot. Italy was not united as a nation until 1861, so although there was a single nationality called "Italian," regionalism, including language, separated them. In fact, in 1949, when the new Saint Cajetan's Church was dedicated on Knox Avenue, the commemorative booklet announced there were 3,500 Italians in Monessen and felt it necessary to break them into regions: Abruzzi, Calabria, Marche, Sicily, Apulia, Campania, and the north.

Those associated with these regions segregated themselves on the streets and in the neighborhoods. The southern Italians, with names like DeRocco, Todaro, and Dodaro, lived primarily on Morgan Avenue. The northern Italians, with names like Bindi, Parigi, Sodi, and Poletini, lived on Ninth Street, Knox, and Chestnut. They even had two clubs. The story goes that early on, the northerners were the dominant Italian group in Monessen and founded the first Italian club called the Italian Society of Mutual Aid. They constructed a building at 601 Third Street. As more immigrants arrived, the northerners became outnumbered by the increasing influx of southerners. In a crucial club vote, the northerners lost. They quit en masse and founded their own club, the North Italian Political Association (NIPA) and built a new club on Knox Avenue. The Mutual Aid built the New Italian Hall on the main street of town and made it one story higher than the NIPA. As late as the 1950s, one businesswoman was denied entrance into the NIPA ladies association, black-balled because she was not a northern Italian. One other club, the Sons of Italy, was founded by returning soldiers from one of the wars.

The Arab world was represented in Monessen by a number of Syrian Christians. Slabey Essey was among the first, selling Maytag washers and later operating a gas station and a restaurant. The Syrians lived in the 100 block of Schoonmaker

*The Saint Michael Syrian Orthodox Church committee poses here with the American flag. From left to right are the following: (front row) P. Nahas, Tom Nahas, Father Mezdelaney, Joseph Moses, and Mike Joseph; (back row) John Daniel, John Kurey, John Haddad, Tony Nahas, Mike Danis, and Sam Austin. (George Essey.)*

Avenue where many sold dry goods. In the Arab cities of the Middle East, such items were sold door-to-door and that is what the Syrians did in Monessen. They would sell goods on credit and, in true Arab fashion, attach no interest. Among these peddlers were Michael Mucy, Tony Nahas, Esper Essey, and Michael Joseph. Michael Simon would eventually run a bus company, which became the Hilltop Bus Company, still in operation today. If people wanted Syrian specialties like *halwah*, a sweet candy, or *hashish*, Syrian herbs, or *burgol*, cracked wheat, they would wait for a peddler from Republic near Uniontown to come to their homes. He would take their orders and travel to Pittsburgh to the stores in the Strip and return with the goodies. The closest bakery for Syrian *baklava* and other pastries was in Mount Lebanon. James Nahas had a small grocery story that eventually stocked items. Often, like the other immigrants, the Syrians made their own specialties like *chunkleash*, a smelly, delicious cheese. The Syrians founded Saint Michael Syrian Orthodox Church at Ninth Street above Knox on June 15, 1913. Before they moved it to Patton Avenue, it was the oldest church in the Antiochian Orthodox Archdiocese of North America.

Less prominent groups also made up a segment of the population. A small French immigration is memorialized by the French Club on Third Street. A few Mexican families survived the purge after World War I. Swedes lived with the Finns in Finntown. A few Serbian families mingled with the Croatians. A single Chinese family ran a laundry on Schoonmaker near Ninth Street.

One prominent Monessen group that is categorized by its religion, rather than its country, is the Jewish community. The first Jew in Monessen was Emmanuel Feldman, who came to the community in 1898 and later opened a meat market at 1014 Morgan Avenue. The Jews bought their baked goods from Rosenblums at Oneida and Schoonmaker and their kosher meat from Levendorff's, which was run by a rabbi. Most of the early Jews settled around Schoonmaker, Donner, and Reed, and their synagogue was located nearby at 153 Schoonmaker between First and Second Streets. Monessen had the largest congregation of Jews in the valley, ultimately totalling 100 to 150 families.

The first three Finns in Monessen, arriving on January 26, 1898, were Johan Raitanen, Kalle Wilberg, and Antti Karki. They were brought to the city because of the Tin Mill and lived in homes provided for them by that company. By 1906, 900 Finns lived in Monessen and in 1919, there were nearly 1,600. Originally settling along Third Street, they soon moved up the hill to what was to become Finntown: Motheral, Clarendon, Chestnut, South Fourth, Sixth, and parts of Knox Avenue. They built private homes and a number of boarding houses that still stand in the area. They also opened two competing co-ops, the Sampo Co-op Association and the Osmo Co-operative, which imported and sold Finnish items like lingonberries for rice pudding, herring that they ate with sour cream, *Lipia Kala*, or dried cod, for Christmas, and cardamom to make the wonderful Finnish *niswa* bread. For other pastry delights, there was Jacob Knuuttilas's bakery at 477 Motheral, where the entire town would go to buy rusk bread. The men would stop to have their hair cut at John Hikkinin's at 523 Fourth Street.

*The Finnish Temperance Hall stood on Fourth Street in Finntown. Home of the Louhi Band, it was torn down in 2001. (Greater Monessen Historical Society.)*

At the two ends of Motheral stood the two minds of the Finns: the Finnish Socialist Hall, sometimes called the Red Hall, with ties to Russia, and the Finnish Temperance Hall, sometimes called the White Hall. Both were huge structures with dynamic architecture. The Socialists had originally built a smaller hall, which they sold to the Sons of Italy on Sixth Street, but they outgrew it and built the larger hall on Clarendon, which was eventually sold and became the Arch Tavern, one of the most famous African-American nightclubs in southwestern Pennsylvania. The other remained a Finnish hall until the 1940s when it was converted into an apartment building. It was torn down by the city in 2001.

The Finns' church, Saint Luke's Evangelical Lutheran Church, was organized on September 10, 1899, in Allenport. In 1900, the church bought one lot and was given a second from the East Side Land Company on Reed Avenue for $420. The Monessen Finnish community was one of the largest communities of Finns in the United States. The closing of the Tin Mill in the 1930s, however, decimated the group, and by 1940, only 172 Finns were in Monessen.

The African-American community came to Monessen for the same reason as everyone else: a better life. They left the South, where discrimination made life almost impossible, and 220,903 people headed north between 1880 and 1910. The mills needed experts to train new employees. Among the first were a group who arrived by train at Webster on July 2, 1901. In that group was James Page, who came to Monessen to work on the expansion of the railroad. He stayed to work at Pittsburgh Steel's wire mill. According to the *Keystone Magazine*, 55 years later, Page was still employed by Pittsburgh Steel. Other prominent "Colored" Monessen families include the Hills, Frezzells, Bartons, Wheelers, Duncans, and Carters.

A few years later, 32 African-American wire drawers came to Monessen from Joliet, Illinois to work for $4 a day, a far higher rate than their American and European counterparts. By 1910, there were 233 blacks in Monessen, and by 1920, that number increased to 588. They settled around Eleventh Street. Most of the community was denied to them, so they settled in and around two multi-unit buildings called Bouquet Flats and Castle Gardens. They found the ingredients for chitterlings and ribs from hucksters and they grew greens and sweet potatoes in small patches of ground around their homes. They set up their own type of discrimination. They judged each other by the same criteria as the whites: color. If an African American could not see the blue vein in the arm, he or she was too black to pass. The lighter and brighter, the better.

African Americans did not cling to any specific department in the mill, but many worked in the wire mill. Wherever there was a job that was too dangerous, too hard, or too demeaning, they got it. As Richard Wright in *The Negro in Pennsylvania* tells us, in 1907, 150 blacks worked as wire drawers, firemen, boiler tenders,

*This picture is of the Frezzell family, one of the African-American families in Monessen. From left to right are (front row) Suzanne and George Thomas; (back row) Ben Thomas Sr., IdaBelle, James Richard, Annie Elizabeth, and mother Elizabeth Alma Northington. The photo was taken by Oscar Stevenson. (IdaBelle Minnie.)*

and laborers at Pittsburgh Steel. These were the dirtiest, most dangerous jobs. African-American workers were often called "strikebreakers"; the truth is that the companies were using them, too. A report by a young man before a United States Senate committee during the strike of 1919 details the following:

> Monessen, November 23, 1919
> Eugene Steward–Age 19–Baltimore, Md.
>
> My native place is Charleston, South Carolina. I arrived in Monesson on Wednesday, November 19. There were about 200 of us loaded in the cars at Baltimore; some were white; and when we were loaded in the cars we were told that we were going to be taken to Philadelphia.
>
> We were not told that a strike was in progress. We were promised $4.00 a day, with the understanding that we should be boarded at $1.00 a day.
>
> When we took the train a guard locked the doors so that we were unable to get out, and no meals were given us on the way, although we were promised board. We were unloaded at Lock 4 and had a guard placed over us, and were then marched into the grounds of the Pittsburgh Steel Products Co. We were then told to go to work, and when I found out that there was a strike on I got out. They refused to let me out at the gate when I protested about working, and I climbed over the fence, and they caught me and compelled me to go back and sign a paper and told me that I would have to go to work. I told them that I would not go to work if they kept me there two years. I was placed on a boat.
>
> There were about 200 other people there. The guards informed me that if I made any attempt to again run away that they would shoot me. I got a rope and escaped, as I will not work to break the strike.
> Eugene X Steward
> mark
> Witness Jacob S. McGinley

One can only imagine their frustration.

The biggest event of the decade did not happen in Monessen at all. It happened far out on the Atlantic Ocean. When the HMS *Titanic's* bow lifted out of the waters of the North Atlantic as if it would touch the sky and then, groaning and screaming, slid beneath the frigid black sea on April 15, 1912, it carried 13 passengers bound for Monessen. They were all Finns. Four more people, Hungarian-Americans bound for Monessen, had been left behind in England. No other community in the world would be asked to carry such a burden. It took awhile for the news to reach Monessen. As the story began to unfold, the first headlines in Monessen inaccurately lamented the loss of a person who was not on the ship at all. But slowly, painfully, over a period of two to three weeks, the horrific tale of the *Titanic's* first and last voyage began to emerge.

# DAILY INDEPENDENT

## MONESSEN, PA., MONDAY, APRIL 22, 1912

### MONS OF SYMPA-THY FOR SEA VICTIMS

tne majority of the sermons de-
d at the local churches yesterday
nces were made to the awful-
er that has thrilled the entire
during the past week, the sink-
f the White Star line steamer
ic.

one knows how soon they may
ummoned by death and this is
ht out all the more clearly when
remembered that a supper at
a large number of guests were
t was being served when all of
en out of an occasion for great
ment came the grim hand of
and swept away with it over
lives. "Nearer, My God To
the strains of which were
by the survivors when the ship
s final plunge into the sea, was
i in almost every church and
were the prayers offered up
the pulpits for the survivors and
rlatives and frends of the dead.
g the other things touched upon
the pre-eminence and supreme-
ty of God, the heroism and self-
ce of those who remained on
the ill fated ship and the
le and inexcusable negligence
steamship company in failing
vide for the safety of their
us burden

### EBALL SEASON OPENED SATURDAY

## FIVE TITANIC SURVIVORS REACH MONESSEN

### Bride of Three Months Widowed---Entire Party in a Highly Nervous State---Band Did Not Play as Ship Sank--Men Cried Pitifully - But Died Bravely

## TWO OF THE PARTY LOSE LIVES

This morning on the 9 o'clock express, Mrs. Hilda Hirvonen and
daughter Hilgur, accompanied by Matt
Hirvonen, the husband and father, and
Mrs. Elin Hakkarainen, a bride of
but three months, Erik Jussila and
Eino Lindquist, arrived here, the former two and last three are survivors
of a party of seven who were passen
gers on the ill fated Titanic which
went down to a watery grave on last
Monday morning at 2 a. m. Mr. Hakkarainen and John Linja are missing
and the report that they were among
those drowned was confirmed on the

arrival of the survivors here.
The entire party is still in an extremely nervous condition after the
harrowing experiences which they
have passed through during the week
and their stories of the disaster will
be recounted in full in tomorrow's
issue of the Independent. Among the
new facts gleaned is the statement
that the band was not playing when
the boat sank but that several people
were playing the pianos in the first
and second cabin sections and that the
men cried pitifully as the boat went
down.

### FIRST DIVIDEND DE-CLARED FOR PINCUS

The creditors of the bank-
Pincus Brothers who formerly o
ated "The Hub" clothing and
nishing store on Schoonmaker aven
opposite the Opera house, were str
dumb today when on opening
morning mail they found checks f
a Pittsburgh law firm for 5 per c
of the amount of their claims, w
the idea faintly interwoven into
polite introductory remarks tha
covered the "first dividend" in
matter of claim against the estate
said Pincus Brothers.

Thus the inference or a faint h
is held out that some time—maybe
the far and uncertain future th
may, possibly, be another divid
declared, but of uncertain amou
supposedly though, even smaller t
the present division. Howe
small favors should be thankfu
received. But to think of it. Th
meek and lowly attorneys, after
decending to tender the enorm
sum of five per cent, deducted th
commission from the poor credit
share, thus making it look like—thi
cents—or there-abouts.

### COLONIAL MINSTREL AT CHARLEROI THIS EVENI

Final rehearsals have been held
everything is in readiness for the
pearance of the Colonial Minstrel
the Turn Verein hall in Charleroi t
evening and tomorrow evening. J
Jenkins, one of the best known a

*An article in the* Monessen Daily Independent *on April 22, 1912 gave details of the sinking of the* Titanic. (Monessen Daily Independent.)

On the evening of April 19, Matt Hirvonen, who worked as a screw boy at mill number 8 of the Tin Mill, got a telegram that his wife, Helga Lindquist Hirvonen, and their daughter were safe, but the remainder of the Monessen-bound Finns were probably drowned. This, too, was incorrect. On April 22, five *Titanic* survivors reached Monessen on the 9 a.m. express train, including Helga and Hildur Hirvonen, Eino Lindquist, Erik Jussila, and Elin Hakkarainen. Monessen began piecing the story together.

Pekka Hakkarainen was among the missing. Hakkarainen had been a tinsmith in the Tin Mill. He had returned to Finland in 1911 for a visit, met Elin, married her, and was bringing her home to 401 Motheral Avenue. They were originally scheduled to sail aboard the RMS *Mauritania,* but they heard the new luxury liner *Titanic* was making its maiden voyage in April, so they changed their plans. The last Elin remembers seeing of him was just after the ship hit the iceberg. He left the cabin to see what was going on.

Marie Panula, her five children, and a companion died as well. Marie's family was separated: the boys in one part of the ship, she and her younger children in the other. She could not gather all her family together and refused to leave the ship until all were found. It cost the lives of the entire family. The Panulas were really bound for Coal Center, but both Coal Center and Monessen were listed as the final destination on the *Titanic's* manifest.

Eino Lindquist reported the following:

> I was a passenger in the third cabin and had been in bed about 2 hours when my room mate and I were awakened by people running to and fro on the deck. We hurriedly dressed ourselves and put on our heaviest clothes and our overcoats, the night being very damp and cold. Going out on the deck we saw the sailors lowering the lifeboats away, filled with women, with men at each end and in the middle to guide and row. My friend, Jussila was called upon to help row one of the boats and I was left alone on the deck.

Hiroven had a ghastly front-row seat to the tragedy. She told the *Charleroi Mail* newspaper what she witnessed:

> I suppose we had been away from the *Titanic* twenty minutes when it went down. I saw it plainly. When it took its final dive people were leaping from all sides into the water. Some of them were saved. When our lifeboat left the *Titanic's* side it was only about half filled. It wasn't long however, before we picked up enough to completely fill it. My brother was found on a raft after we had been six and a half hours at sea.

Elin Hakkarainen offers an even more graphic view of the sinking, printed in the booklet *I'm Going to See What has Happened,* written by her son and co-writer Janet White. The story recounts the following:

> The scene that I now witnessed was forever etched in my memory. I would never forget the sounds that came from the *Titanic* at this time. As the stern of the ship rose higher and higher, everything within the ship broke loose and went crashing downward to the bow. There was a mad rush of passengers and crew to the rear of the well and poop decks. There seemed to be a mad rush of people from below. The locked doors that I had encountered must have been opened at the last moment. Many hundreds more must have been trapped below decks and crushed by the breaking up of the ship. One of the giant funnels toppled to the deck crushing many passengers at it slid into the water. The screaming and moaning of the trapped passengers was beyond description. The *Titanic* was standing straight up, the three huge propellers glistened in the starlight. We were all hypnotized by the sight of the giant ship

standing on end, going down slowly, ever so slowly, as if an invisible hand was holding it back. Hundreds of people were holding on to the railings, stairs and ladders, capstans and framework of the rear docking bridge. The ship's lights, which had remained on during the entire episode, finally went out.

Catherine Torkos and her three children, Mary, Michael, and Elizabeth, were also scheduled to sail on the *Titanic*. They were headed for Monessen where Joseph Torkos, husband and father, was working as a wire puller at the Pittsburgh Steel Company. Through a series of events, they ended up on a different ship and spent a fretful voyage crossing the Atlantic in the wake of the *Titanic,* expecting to see a similar fate, while their father, back in Monessen, suffered in silence what he thought was the loss of his family.

The Torkos family survived on the high seas through a mischievous prank. Michael hit his sister Mary, causing her to fall on a rock pile and badly scratch her cheek. In 1912, there were no antibiotics, so Mary was forbidden to board the *Titanic* for fear that she would spread infection. They were left behind to sail a few days later on the *Kortland*. However, as Joseph Torkos worked at Pittsburgh Steel, he thought that his family was gone. The family made their way to Monessen without fanfare. There was no assistance, no news reporters to greet them. In fact, they did not know what to do when they reached Monessen. Mary explained their arrival:

> We arrived at the train station and did not know where to go. My father was not there to meet us. So we asked a stranger for help. He asked us if we knew where my father lived. We didn't. He asked us if we knew where my father worked. That we knew. He worked at Pittsburgh Steel. The man took us to the gate where they told us to wait. They went looking for my father who was working at the time, but he would not come. He told them, "You have the wrong person, my family was all lost on the *Titanic*."

# 3. WAR, PESTILENCE, AND DENIAL
## A DECADE OF TERROR

Monessen was still in its infancy when a number of cataclysmic events took place, rattling the small community to its foundations: World War I, the Spanish influenza epidemic, Prohibition, and the great steel strike of 1919. For a community that was still trying to define itself and find common ground, it was a seesaw ride of frustration and fear. War and pestilence bound the community together, while Prohibition and labor conditions divided it once again.

Pittsburgh Steel was still expanding. There was a new tube mill. By August of 1913, the newly built, state-of-the-art blast furnaces were up and running and Pittsburgh Steel led the industry in daily and monthly production of iron. In 1914, Pittsburgh Steel expanded its open hearth department and four more furnaces went on line. More furnaces meant more men, and men meant families, and families needed housing, so the boom continued.

The Tin Mill had become the American Tin Plate Company, then the American Sheet and Tin Plate Company's National Works. Its biggest item was the tin can. In the early part of this century, the tin can was a miracle. At first, it was used only for oil and preserved fruit, but as the mills like Monessen improved and changed, innovations made the list of foods continue to grow. Soon, fruits and vegetables of all kinds, condensed milks, hair products, and automotive products were poured and sealed into the 98-percent steel and 2-percent tin containers. A Monessen tin can could go to Alaska, for example, where fishermen canned fish to be eaten at any time in any place in the world.

In town, a new viaduct over Third Street linked two of Monessen's many hills. No sooner was it in use than the good citizens of Third Street were complaining that they were being pelted with debris and wanted something done about it. The men who gathered in the flourishing and abundant hotels and bars in Monessen would drink White Ribbon Beer, the specialty of the house made by the Monessen Brewery, a shining example of small enterprise. The Philadelphia Candy Kitchen opened for business to the tunes of a 15-piece coronet band on June 14, 1912. All over town, the various ethnic clubs were being built. Monessen had a new theater in 1915 to keep the Star company—the Olympic, at 475 Donner Avenue. Eventually, the theater would become the Manos. In 1920, T.S. Laforte opened the Monessen Music Store. By 1920, despite the turmoil of the decade, Monessen was the number one town in Westmoreland County and it was still growing.

It is now fairly well accepted that World War I, the Great War, was so badly fought that millions of men died because of poor tactics on the part of their generals. Throwing men against the German line day after day, week after week, and year after year led to the greatest slaughter of human beings in history. But the men of Monessen honored the call to war. Everyone answered the call: the "Americans," the "Foreigners," and the "Coloreds." Some of the immigrants still did not speak English at the time and most of them were not United States citizens. Most of the men from southwestern Pennsylvania were part of the 80th Division of the First Army, the Blue Ridge Division, which included men from Virginia and West Virginia. It was organized at Camp Lee and headed for France in May of 1918. During the war, the 80th Division lost 1,141 men, had 5,622 wounded, and 101 taken prisoner. The division's men were awarded 42 Distinguished Service Crosses.

The letters the men wrote home provide an image of the war. Private Joseph Lescanac of Battery Company 315 F AAEF left Monessen on April 27, 1918 and later wrote to the *Daily Independent* to tell folks that he had seen action all over France. Robert McKelvie received a letter from his brother James that Monessen

*This fascinating interior picture of Pittsburgh Steel Company's tube mill, c. 1915, shows not only the early machinery, but the primitive working conditions as well. (Raymond Johnson II/Greater Monessen Historical Society.)*

boys were asked to "parade in Paris with President Wilson and his entourage." They were given this honor in lieu of their 17 days in the Bois d'Agone where they took an "active part in the big smash of November 1."

Corporal Homer J. Margerum wrote a letter to his father, John, on Father's Day because he was "only too glad to have a Father to write to." Margerum told his father and, through him, told the good folks of Monessen, where he had been. It sounded horrific. Six submarines had attacked the five troop ships of his group as they were crossing the Atlantic on their way to war. From May 25 to June 28, his unit fought in the front line at Belleau Woods. They were given a rest until July 5 when they joined the drive from the River Marne to the River Vesle at Tismes. He was at Verdun and at the Grandpre in the Argonne Woods. His letter describes the following:

> I got mustard gassed on Oct 21st and have been in the base hospital since at Mevers, France. I was burned pretty bad about the body and eyes, but I am recovering fast and I consider myself very lucky in getting off this light. Just try to imagine thousands of shells going over your head bursting alongside you and millions of machine bullets passing you up, one pounders, 75, 77, 88, 155, 210, 320, big caliber guns and hundreds of airplanes over your head dropping bombs, and steel falling like hell and we fellows coming out as we did, don't you think we were lucky? To tell the truth, I never expected to see the U.S. again, but I see now that my chances are good.

Industrially, Monessen was ready for World War I. Its sluggish mills burst into production and sales to the military soared, but the constant stream of workers from Europe had been cut off. A new work force was needed. Some ethnic women complied, but more often, Mexicans and African Americans replaced the depleting workforce. They were recruited the same way that many of the immigrants had been recruited, via agents who would travel south to hire them. Pittsburgh Steel used this system. Once in Monessen, the recruits were housed in special barracks erected in Wireton and they never left the mill grounds. This influx of African Americans increased their population in Monessen from 1.9 percent in 1910 to 3.2 percent in 1920. The Products Company gave bronze medals to the men who stayed behind and worked in the mill; 1,000 medals were given to men who worked for 90 days without a day off. When the war was over, Pittsburgh Steel welcomed 700 employees back by offering them their old jobs and firing the Mexicans and African Americans who had replaced them.

The tenor of life in the community changed, too. Conservation was asked of every citizen. If you ate peaches, Mrs. Motz asked you to save the pits and donate them to the war effort where they would be turned into carbon for gas masks. Uncle Sam asked for money to pay for the war in a series of Liberty Bond drives. The bonds became barter both during and after the war. Ads in local newspapers said that by buying goods with Liberty Bonds, consumers would receive change

*This is the order of march for the parade held on July 4, 1919, to welcome the men home from the war. Every band, every ethnic club joined the parade that lasted for hours and filled the streets of Monessen from one end of town to the other. It is typical of the type of parades held during this time.* (Monessen News.)

**Line of Parade
July 4, 1919**

FIRST DIVISION
Com W. D. Hunter
Form on Donner at Oneida
Executive Committee
Louhi Finnish Band
Civil War Vets in autos
Soldiers, Sailors, & Marines
Monessen Vol Fire Department

———

SECOND DIVISION
Com Capt J. E. Newcomer
Form Schoon, west of 1st
General Committee
Pittsburgh Steel Product Co. Band
Monessen Board of Trade
Merchants
Citizens

———

THIRD DIVISION
Com Carl Woodward
Form Donner & 1st
New Eagle Band
B.P.O.E. Lodge 773
Knights of Columbus Lodge 954
McKeesport Drum Corps
Sons & Daughters of St George
Additional groups

———

FOURTH DIVISION
Com Eli Wolf
Form Schoon & 2nd
Italian Citizen's Band
Italian Benevolent Society
Italian Civic Society
Franco-Belgium Society

———

FIFTH DIVISION
Com J. I. Smith
Form Donner & 2nd
Charleroi Slovak Band

Monessen Slovak Band
Pennsylvania Slovak Yednots
Czecho-Slovak League
Slovak Gymanstic Sokol
Slovak Catholic Yednots
Slovak Catholic Sokol
National Slovak Society
Indepdendent Political Club
Croatian Beneficial Slovok
Greek Slovak Sojedeninia
Russian Orthodox Society

SIXTH DIVISION
J.H. Watt
Form 3rd & Schoon
Monessen Polish Band
Polish Falcons
Polish Musical
Young Ladies Catholic Falcons
All other Polish societies

———

SEVENTH DIVISION
C. H. Williams
Form 3rd & Donner
Labelle Band
Monessen Drum Corps
American-Greek and all
Greek societies

———

EIGHTH DIVISION
Com Harry Lebowitz
Form 4th & Schoon
Monessen Hungarian Band
Hungarian Societies

LINE OF MARCH
Donner to Oneida, Sheneca to
Schoonmaker, Schoonmaker to
10th, 10th to Donner, thence to the
subwy and disband at Electric
Park.
Parade committee
J. J. Cushing, Chairman.

From the **Monessen News** July 3, 1919.

in cash. (Stores also admonished Monessenites to "Buy Monessen" and stop spending money in other towns.)

On April 24, 1917, the first Liberty Loan Drive was held. Five such drives from April 1917 to August 1919 kept the people dipping into their savings. As each drive began, there was a parade. John Phillip Sousa had written a special march called the "Liberty Loan March" and the people walked to its beat. These parades were a prelude to all the parades to follow. When the American Red Cross created the Monessen–Belle Vernon Chapter on June 24, 1917, they had several parades. When the men began coming home after the Armistice of November 1918, Monessen had a large, welcoming Fourth of July parade. Water buckets were set along the routes of these gigantic parades so participants could get a drink of water.

As much as there were things to bind the community together, there were things that separated it once again. Russia was in the midst of revolution. Europe was at war. The United States government was paranoid and started looking around at all the immigrants in the country, on the look-out for "anarchists,"

THIRD
LIBERTY LOAN
SUBSCRIBER

*Throughout the Liberty Loan drives, folks who donated to the cause would place signs like this in their windows. (Greater Monessen Historical Society.)*

"Bolsheviks," "communists," and any other group it considered radical, including feminists. The Senate and Congress enacted a series of laws that not only violated the constitutional rights of these groups, but focused primarily on ethnic cultures. Immigrants, whether they were naturalized or not, were the objects of the Espionage Act, the Sedition Act, and the Palmer raids.

The Espionage Act of 1917 came first, permitting the government to go after immigrants and bring them to the ground. They could be arrested if they said anything that could be interpreted as anti-American. They could go to jail if they refused to serve in the United States Army. The Sedition Act of 1918 followed. It expanded on the Espionage Act and led directly to the Palmer raids, which were the insurance policy that made the two acts work. Named for the attorney general, they were carried out by a special police force that looked for and raided the homes and clubs of potential anarchists or terrorists, spreading panic in the hearts of people throughout the country. The raids turned into witch hunts.

In point of fact, anarchists and communists were a reality in the United States. The Pittsburgh area was considered to be the center of the "red" rebellion. Various types of meetings were held in Monessen, Bentleyville, McKees Rocks, Charleroi, Ellsworth, California, and the small coal patches in northern West Virginia. Pittsburgh's leading spokesman was a man named Jacob Margolis, an attorney and leader of the Industrial Workers of the World (IWW), otherwise known as "Wobblies." Charles H. McCormick, in his outstanding book *Seeing Reds*, claims,

"Federal agents believed that this organization was part of a secret conspiracy behind much of the labor agitation and antiwar activity in the Pittsburgh mill district." The IWW, started by the likes of Eugene Debs and Mother Jones, became tainted by innuendo and, although it began as a socialist organization trying to help labor and to right wrongs, the IWW became stained by government propaganda and turned radical.

At the same time, the Italian anarchists believed any government was corrupt and, therefore, there should be no government at all. Sacco and Vanzetti were the most famous anarchists in the United States. These two Italian immigrants, in one of the country's most famous cases of injustice, were tried and put to death for a crime they did not commit. Such were the times; such was the prejudice. Most of the Mon Valley anarchists lived in Black Diamond, Gallatin, and Millsboro, and a few were scattered through the other valley towns. When these anarchist groups turned violent and began bombing prominent places and people around the country, Palmer swung into action. In August of 1919, Donora was targeted and over 100 people were arrested.

Agent Fred Ames, a former Pennsylvania State Constabulary at Greensburg and a member of the Radical Squad of the federal government, led the raids in Monessen. Ames had planted a spy among the Russians in Monessen and had found the potential enemies. In addition to the federal forces, Ames organized the state police and the Pittsburgh Steel Coal and Iron Police for the raids. They began on a Saturday morning in November of 1919 and did not end until early Sunday morning. Surely people bolted their doors and turned off their lights, hoping this plague would pass them by. The raids must have reminded some immigrants of the ethnic cleansing that had taken place in Europe, the reason they had come to the United States in the first place. By the time the raid was finished, 20 Monessenites were in jail.

The majority of the Monessen "aliens" were Russians, and they were arrested at a pool hall at Schoonmaker and Eleventh Street. The owner had been arrested earlier. They mostly lived on Highland and Twelfth Street. They were charged as "being members of the Russian Workers Organization, one of the most feared in America." The United States government maintained that this group planned to overthrow the government. Officials believed that the organization had over 7,000 members nationwide and that the current raids were against its leaders. The men were taken to Greensburg to stand trial. One man proudly stood and said he was "an anarchist pure and simple." That was enough to deport him. Fourteen more were found guilty and sentenced to deportation. In December, a special train left Pittsburgh bound for Ellis Island and, guilty or not, they were gone.

The returning soldiers brought back an unwelcome guest to Monessen when they returned from the battlefields of Europe in 1918. It was the deadly Spanish influenza. Monessen seemed to be beating the disease, but then, on October 14, the city held yet another parade to celebrate the end of the war. The usual 10,000 people attended from all over the valley, coughing on one another as they stood three and four deep along the sidewalks of the city. It was not long before volunteers began supervising the community effort to fight the sickness. H. Dallas McCabe, still head of the East Side Land Company, was in charge. Ray Motz, suffragette and businesswoman, took care of supplies. By mid-October, the Elks Lodge on Seventh Street was commandeered by the Red Cross as a hospital. Schools closed on October 21. On October 22, confectionery stores, soda fountains, soft drink vendors, and ice cream venders were forbidden to serve "in house." All sales had to be "take away."

Nothing could stop the spread. The death rate was rising and obituaries were posted on the front page of the *Daily Independent* if one was "American," or listed on page four if one was "Foreign" or "Colored." By October 23, teachers were required to work as volunteers, going about the community looking for the sick and trying to improve health conditions. The hospitals were looking for cots. The following day, a daily death record was posted. At this point, the Elks hospital was closed and the patients moved to larger quarters at the high school. The ethnic women from the community began reporting to the high school to help nurse the sick, bringing with them their age-old folk medicines. The tenements and poorer sections of town were the hardest hit. Entire families lay prostrate with fever and fear. Neighbors were helping neighbors. On October 29, the Pittsburgh Steel Products Company opened a hospital for its employees in Turner Hall at Donner and Second Street.

*The Elks Lodge on Seventh Street was used as a hospital during the Spanish flu epidemic. Today, it is the home of the Mon Valley Retired Steelworkers (MARS). The building originally cost $50,000 and was first occupied on November 16, 1914. (Greater Monessen Historical Society.)*

# CLOSED

## FOR VIOLATION OF

# NATIONAL PROHIBITION ACT

### BY ORDER OF

## UNITED STATES DISTRICT COURT

———— DISTRICT OF ————

## All persons are forbidden to enter premises without order from the UNITED STATES MARSHAL

*If a business violated the law against drinking, it was shut down and this sign was posted on its door by the federal government. (Greater Monessen Historical Society.)*

On November 26, the quarantine was lifted, and by the end of November, the ban on hotels, bars, theaters, and churches was lifted. The hospitals closed shortly thereafter, and, for all intents and purposes, by December 1, the influenza was over in Monessen. The *Monessen News* reported on November 26 that people between the ages of 30 and 40 were hit hardest; many did not die of the influenza itself, however, but of pneumonia. The emergency hospital at the high school treated 282 patients: 169 males, 113 females, 102 married, 180 single, 279 white, and 3 African American (which raises a number of questions). The official death toll for the entire community, posted in the *Daily* on December 10, stood at 226. Surely it was higher, as there were many who died before or after the peak time when the special hospitals were open, and many unreported cases existed among the immigrants and African Americans.

Temperance proponents had been hard at work for decades in Monessen, but had little effect until the country was swept up in extremes. Today, some historians argue that Prohibition was a last-ditch attempt by the "Americans" to hold on to the country's power and morals and stem the tide of the rising ethnic melting pot. There is a lot of truth to that and we can still see evidence of it today, but in Monessen in this decade, one of the largest temperance organizations was Finnish.

On April 8, 1919, the *Monessen News-Call* announced the thundering news that Westmoreland County would go dry. There would be no booze in Monessen,

*Prohibition also hurt the economy. The Monessen Brewery never reopened after it was forced to shut down. Marginal at best, it was the largest building in Monessen and was eventually torn down. (Greater Monessen Historical Society.)*

no *Dago* Red, no Greek *Mustika*, no Russian white lightning. It was devastating news for the small breweries and distilleries in the valley. The Firestone (once Monessen) Distilling Company went out of business and disappeared from memory. The Monessen Brewery's huge 5-story building, with the enormous tower that loomed over the river, remained a hulk of empty memories for decades. No more White Ribbon Beer in the Mon Valley, no more Monongahela Rye, and no more jobs. All along the Monongahela, small breweries and distilleries closed and their entrepreneurial-type business would not reopen in the United States until the 1990s.

The demise of one of the leading purveyors in the country, the Gibsonton Distillery, was more devastating. Sitting on Route 906 on the outskirts of the city, Gibsonton was one of the most famous distillers in the United States. In 1856, John Gibson purchased over 40 acres to build a distillery on the east bank of the Monongahela River. Limestone was hewn out of the nearby Gibson Quarry and the cornerstone was put in place. When the contractors were finished, the site contained eight bonded warehouses, a 4-story malt house, a distillery, millhouse, drying kiln, saw mill, boiler, two carpenter shops, a cooper shop, a blacksmith shop, and an ice house.

Gibsonton began making rye whiskey in April of 1857. According to George Dallas Albert's *History of the County of Westmoreland Pennsylvania*, printed in 1882, "There is no distillery in America that has such costly and substantial buildings, and none that equals it in the purity and flavor of its whiskeys, which have a world-wide reputation for their excellence." The thirst for this alcoholic brew was felt as far as the West Indies, France, England, the Philippines, and even China, not to mention all over the United States. At the business's peak, 5,000 railroad cars loaded with whiskey-filled barrels were shipped yearly from the distillery.

They manufactured 150 barrels of whiskey a day at a value of $80 a barrel. The company paid an estimated $750,000 in taxes each year, or $2,000 a day, a lot of revenue lost to the bootleggers.

Once Prohibition began, the Gibson Distillery went bankrupt. On Tuesday, September 8, 1923, a sheriff's sale was held and when it was over, nothing remained of the distillery except the buildings. The Pittsburgh Steel Company acquired the property. In 1926, the limestone buildings were dismantled and the blocks were sold at $1 a load. People from all over the Mon Valley purchased the locally quarried stone for their own use. Many a valley building or wall has a bit of the distillery in it. The Belle Vernon newspaper *The Enterprise* reported the following:

> It is said the Trinity Protestant Episcopal Church of Monessen [688 Reed] will use a large portion of the stone in erecting a building in that city . . . I wonder if these stones, which once housed whiskey, will save as many souls as the contents sent to hell.

The demise of alcohol was no less overwhelming to the clubs in Monessen. It was an economic hardship, an example of why Prohibition was looked on as politically motivated. The clubs' livelihood depended on their beverage revenues. Many fell into financial trouble. Buildings had mortgages. Income, without alcohol, was slim. Some began to bootleg. Individuals lost not only

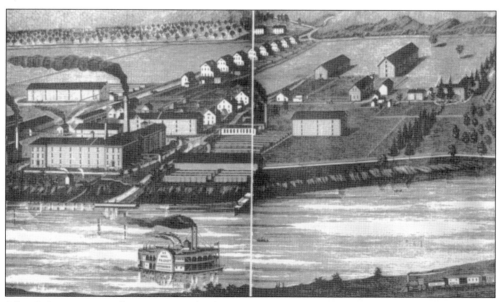

*The Gibsonton Distillery just outside of Monessen was put out of business by Prohibition. Its warehouses were dismantled, but its homes were moved across the highway to the hills beyond. They still stand. (Greater Monessen Historical Society.)*

their livelihood, but their pleasure. Hundreds of Italians made wine in their basements. It was nothing to see dozens of trucks laden with California grapes coming into the community each October from the docks at the Strip District in Pittsburgh. The *Daily Independent* reported in 1919 that thousands of pounds of grapes had been confiscated from those trucks as Prohibition destroyed tradition. All together, hundreds, if not thousands, of jobs were lost from Pittsburgh to Brownsville. No industry came along to replace the brewery and distillery businesses in the Mon Valley.

A law only works if the citizens obey it, and this law, like the gambling and prostitution laws, was destined to be broken. In 1920, bars all over Westmoreland County were still selling liquor and beer over the counter. The police had a hard time keeping up with them, so the Monessen bootlegger was born. Monessen had stills all over town. There was one on the steps between Fourth and Third Street, several on Highland Avenue, and more on Schoonmaker. As late as 1929, the Sheetz Hotel was ordered padlocked for one year for violations of the Volsted Act. Prohibition would plague Monessen for the next 40 years. It was the incubator of organized crime and corrupt politicians, who would rise to power and dominate life in Monessen.

Into all this chaos came the working men seeking a better way of life. The timing could not have been worse. The events surrounding the decade were perfect vehicles to slant public opinion against the workers. From the beginning, the strike of 1919 was doomed to failure. Legitimate strikers, aiming at a better life, were bunched together with the anarchists and communists. It was a formula for defeat.

Monessen, as would become the pattern, was divided according to interests. The majority of the "Americans" did not want the strike, since they were mostly businessmen, who depended on a good economy, and mill bosses, who sided with the company. African Americans did not want the strike either. Although many held legitimate jobs in the mills, they would be accused as strikebreakers. In addition, the African-American community did not want to join a union that had not supported them in the past. (The Amalgamated pressured them to join and some did.) These groups constituted the two extremes in the town.

The European immigrants, on the other hand, were fighting for decent wages and benefits. The Italians, Poles, Finns, Ukrainians, Russians, Hungarians, Slavs, Croatians, and Greeks wanted better working hours and safer mills. The union gave them a power they did not think they could have in the United States. The immigrants were going on strike against the railroads, the coal barons, and the auto industry. There is no doubt about it, it was a worker's revolution.

The war, combined with the strike, made the immigrants strong. One of the many company spies in Monessen during the strike would report the following to Pittsburgh Steel:

> The principal topic of conversation and of complaint among the men
> is, that now they are being called Foreigners, Hunkies, Wops, Pollocks,

*An interior view shows Pittsburgh Steel Company's wire mill as it was in 1915. Note the lack of safety equipment. (Raymond Johnson II/Greater Monessen Historical Society.)*

etc., but that during the war they had all been considered 100 per cent American, when they worked long hours, subscribed to Liberty Bonds, Red Cross, Y M C A Salvation Army Relief, Jewish Relief and all such war contributions, when they responded to every call and every demand that was made on them, and even went overseas to fight for freedom and democracy. They resent now being called Foreigners and to be deprived of the privilege of free speech, the right of assembly . . . X-199.

He hit the nail on the head. The country was never to have it both ways again.

The strongest union at the time was the Amalgamated Association of Iron, Steel, and Tin Workers, a leftover from earlier days. The Amalgamated formed groups of men called "Flying Squads" to go into the mill towns to organize. In the spring of 1919, the Amalgamated sent such squads all over western Pennsylvania, including to Monessen. At the same time, the companies were implementing squads of their own. They organized undercover agents to infiltrate among the workers and spy on them. These agents, some put in place a year before the strike occurred, were either directly employed by the companies to work in the mills, or they were hired from agencies to mingle with the men in public and get information.

The strike took a long time to manifest itself. Amalgamated's national committee met on July 20, 1919 and adopted 12 demands. These demands form the heart and soul of labor's struggles from as early as the 1880s to the 1930s:

The right of collective bargaining.

Reinstatement of all men discharged for union activities with pay for time lost.

The eight hour day.

One day's rest in seven.

Abolition of the 24 hour shift.

Increase in wages sufficient to guarantee American standard of living.

Standard scales of wages in all trades and classifications of workers.

Double rates of pay for all overtime after 8 hours, holiday and Sunday work.

Check off system of collecting union dues and assessments.

Principles of seniority to apply in the maintenance reduction and increase of working forces.

Abolition of company unions.

Abolition of physical examination of applicants for employment.

*Ads like this one appeared in newspapers throughout the steel belt. They were written in various languages and contained company propaganda designed to confuse the workers and make them return to work. They worked!*

No newspaper in southwestern Pennsylvania aired the grievances of the men who worked in the mills. In fact, the newspapers were on the side of the mills and they were just as eager to throw fallacy around. Newspapers, including the *Daily Independent,* wanted the men back at work. The Monessen Board of Trade joined in the conspiracy, too. On September 29, 1919, Pittsburgh's *Sun* newspaper placed the board on record as claiming that wages and living conditions of Monessen's mill workers were good. They maintained "that the workmen in the steel industry have been better paid than other occupations for similar service and that they have lived just as well as they knew how or desired."

The truth was a bit different. Wages were dependent on nationality and skin color. Workers that were native born of a native father earned $17.81 a week. African Americans in the same category earned $14.82. According to the United States Congress Senate Reports of the Immigration Commission, native-born workers of a foreign father were paid based on where the father was born. The highest paid workers in that category were from France at $20.79 a week. The lowest of this category was Austro-Hungary at $12.77. The average was around $17. The final category included people who had just arrived in the country. English ($18.80), Scotch ($19.01), or Welsh ($22.15) immigrants earned the most in this category, while the Slovenians ($11.89), Northern Italians ($12.01), Southern Italians ($11.83), and Greeks ($11.85) earned the least. All of them worked 12 hours a day, enduring 24-hour turn around shifts, and had no health and retirement benefits.

In an effort to avoid the steel strike, President Woodrow Wilson tried to bring the two sides together for talks. One man stood in the way: Judge Elbert Gary, head of U.S. Steel. At first, Gary refused to meet, a ploy that has been used in negotiations ever since. He insisted that 85 percent of the workers did not want to strike, but this was not true. The National Committee's reaction was to fix the strike date for September 22, 1919. On September 18, Pittsburgh Steel closed its doors to workers, constituting an illegal lock-out. Close to 100 workers paraded through downtown in a show of strength. The other Monessen mills followed Pittsburgh Steel's example. More men were out of work. Early on September 23, nearly 2,000 steel men gathered in Monessen and marched along the newly constructed Webster Road to Donora.

On the same day, Burgess Stewart issued a proclamation that forbade unauthorized meetings and parades, also an illegal act. (It was the second time such a decree was issued. On April 1, the union tried to hold an organizational meeting in Monessen. Miners from out of town came to Monessen to join the protest. The burgess tried to forbid gatherings, but he lost, and Monessen was considered an open town.) The burgess further announced the closure of all clubs and forbade the sale of alcohol. In order to create fear, Pittsburgh Steel paid all of its workers in full as if it were about to shut down for good. The next day, September 24, the burgess called a meeting at the high school auditorium to explain his position and the new rules in Monessen. The truth of the matter was that the burgess used the proclamation at his own whim. In investigating

*The Pittsburgh Steel Products Company Iron and Coal Police were a legitimate police force approved by the Pennsylvania legislator. Organized throughout the Pittsburgh Coal Seam, they were feared in the communities they served, often being called "Yellow Dogs" or "Cossacks." The Pennsylvania governor eliminated them in 1930. (Greater Monessen Historical Society.)*

the strike, the Interchurch World Movement, a consortium of various religious leaders who studied the steel strike in 1920, concluded with the following:

> This proclamation, while strictly enforced against the strikers, was not enforced in other cases, as certain workers were permitted to meet for the purpose of discussing a petition to return to work, and large meetings in behalf of the League of Nations.

On September 24, Donora strikers attempted to return the compliment and march on Monessen. This created a confrontation that could have turned into a disaster. The *Daily Independent* reported the incident in detail. The burgess created a 500-man Citizens Protective League to protect the community. Many of the volunteers were former soldiers of World War I. Stewart knowingly tried to recruit leaders from the various ethnic groups in town, but he did not often succeed and ended up with too many African Americans. The league members were issued guns and formed into companies and were asked to gather at the borough building, at Fourth Street and Donner, on the day of the march. Five hundred men showed up. The state police from Greensburg took a portion of the group to patrol the streets to stop the citizens from gathering. Others were to follow 16 mounted Coal and Iron Police (the "Cossacks" or "Yellow Dogs") to Donora to stop the marchers. The newspaper reported the following:

> The members of the Citizens Protective League were taken to the Athletic [Page or Electric] Park and formed into their companies while the ex-soldiers met in the borough building. They were furnished with riot guns and formed into columns of two, under the leadership of three former officers of the World War. They marched down Donner Avenue to the subway [Tube Street] where they met the members of the Citizens Protective League and all were sent to the borough limits at the lower end of town.

When the police reached the Donora marchers, they had already crossed the Monongahela and were near Webster. There was a bit of an altercation and the marchers returned to Donora.

Five hundred armed men given extraordinary power can get into a heap of trouble and they did. Hundreds of men were patrolling the streets of Monessen looking for agitators. Incident after incident was reported in the newspaper.

*The Monessen police force was also overwhelmed by events of the decade. Pictured here in 1914 are three officers: Chief of Police John Wheatley, Matt Rautio (left), and John Acton. (Mrs. Frew/Greater Monessen Historical Society.)*

*This picture shows a long view of the Tin Mill as it looked in 1908 when it had been up and running for a number of years. Little is mentioned in the newspapers of strike activities at the mill, but, as with all Monessen mills, the Tin Mill was in turmoil. (Greater Monessen Historical Society.)*

People were shot for tearing down posters from telegraph poles. Twenty people were arrested one day, two on another. People rebelled. One woman from McMahon threw pepper at an officer and was taken to jail. People began breaking windows and causing disturbances. The following was reported in the *Amalgamated Journal*:

> The burgess swore in as deputies all the men he could find, mostly negroes . . . . Sometimes they [the deputies] would search a fellow for weapons, and if he happened to have some money they would take it from him and [even] threaten to shoot him.

The vigilantes were described as a "reign of terror" from the "riff raff of Monessen."

When the strike was over, the Senate Committee on Education and Labor looked at these events and called Monessen residents in for questioning before a notary public in an attempt to see if their civil rights were violated. Concetta Scudieri Cocchiara was one of the immigrant women in question. She resided at 1008 Morgan Avenue and was eight months pregnant at the time of the deposition. The following was written of her trial:

> Policeman followed her and forced himself into the house and struck [her] with a stick on the head and grabbed her by the hair and pulled

her from the kitchen to the outside and forced her into the patrol wagon taking her to the Borough Jail . . . . [She had] no opportunity to call witnesses . . . [and was] pronounced "guilty" and sentenced to a fine and costs amounting to $9.80.

Other Monessen citizens were also interviewed by the Senate committee. John Komer of 265 Schoonmaker Avenue, a 24-year citizen of the United States, heard shots on November 10 around 8 p.m. He got up from his kitchen table and went outside to see what was happening. He was struck with a gun and his eye almost popped out. His wife came out to help him. She was struck and kicked. Komer was dragged to the police station. The burgess fined Komer $10. Paul Yagodisch of 16 Bridge Street in Wireton stopped along Aberdeen Avenue to talk to three friends at about 11 p.m. on October 21. He was arrested. He refused to go to the police station, saying he had done nothing wrong. He was kicked, hit with an iron pipe, and deliberately cut with a knife. He was fined $12.48 and put on trial for resisting arrest.

It was also disclosed after the strike that throughout 1919, Pittsburgh Steel kept a "labor file" with over 600 reports from special agents that they had enlisted. Once these reports were read, lists of men would be circulated among the industry in the Mon Valley as undesirable or black-listed, not to be hired. Blacklists were compiled haphazardly. Anyone could turn in a name and it would be acted upon. The Pittsburgh Steel Products Company received a list of names from an anonymous worker on a dirty piece of yellow paper. The names were not only added to the Products Company blacklist, but were sent off to every other mill in Monessen: Page's, the Foundry, the Tin Mill, and Pittsburgh Steel. The men were finished in the town. No one checked to see if this was a grudge list by an angry man, such was the tenor of the times.

The other mills did not want unionization either. As far back as 1898, Donner had created (and patented) a system of handling tin that became known as the Monessen System. It increased production by continuously rolling tin, which in turn reduced the number of men needed to roll the material by hand. According to Mike Workman in *A History of Pittsburgh Steel Company's Monessen Works*, "Such a system could have emerged only under non union conditions." Hence, the Tin Mill had ample reason to fight the unions.

The spy system set up by the mills was shocking. It was devised to terrorize the community and it did. Where once trust existed within ethnic groups, this system attacked that base as well. A family was truly on its own. At a time when a war had been waged, diseases had killed so many, and people were being accused of being "Reds," one more pestilence must have been extremely difficult to endure. One of the most prolific of the spies in Monessen was a person referred to as Z-16, but there were others operating in the community: X-199, 203, 103, and 150. In fact, Agent 150's sole job in Monessen was to follow and report on a Monessen woman named Anie Witewqitch, a widow considered to be a dangerous radical. In a report, Agent 150 said the following:

> Dear Sir:
>
> There is a widow lady by name Anie Witewqitch at 107 Forest Str. Monessen, PA. living by kindless support of _____ Co., Monessen, Pa. Her Husband Hawrile Witowitch From his careleslee fault was killed un the Mills of said Company about a year ago.
>
> On the first place this lady is not American citizen but an instigator and Bolshevik part foreigner.
>
> She not takes care of her children nor home, but leaves the house uncleaned and children unwashed, uncombed, hungry, craying day after day and herself run around neighbor women carrying tales, gossips, slanders and lies from one to the other making them angry, mad at each other make them quareling and suit, she is a regular instigator.

The spies were everywhere. They got rooms in the boarding houses. They got jobs in the mills. They listened and reported all that they saw and heard to the company. X-199 was a Slavic operative and he found a room with Mrs. MacKinzie at 160 First Street. Her husband and father worked in the tube mill and the man befriended them and reported all they said back to the mill. He happily reported that at one union meeting, the Slavic speaker said "that he was making use of his native tongue so that the detectives present at the meeting would not understand what he was saying." They also tried to agitate and create conflict in the community. Z-16 said the following:

> A woman in the post office asked a fellow today to go with her and cash a Liberty Bond as her money was all gone and the children in the house wanted shoes. I got next to her and told her she should not sell her Liberty Bond, but she explained she really needed money and was obliged to do so. She explained that none of her boarders were working, yet she still keeps them, but I advised her to tell those fellows to go to work or else throw them out, but she wouldn't do that to any one, saying, "I had those boys before and I will keep them now."

On October 6, 1919, in a turn-around, Pittsburgh Steel opened its gates to workers. That same day, a meeting was held in Washington, D.C. at President Wilson's request. It consisted of representatives of labor, industry, and the public. The infamous Judge Gary attended the meetings, not as an employer and president of U.S. Steel, but as a member of the general public. After haggling and bargaining for days, followed by a presidential plea, they were able to present the following statement:

> The right of wage earners to organize without discrimination, to bargain collectively, to be represented by representatives of their own choosing in negotiations and adjustments with employers in respect to wages, hours of labor, and relations and conditions of employment, is recognized.

*The P&LE train station at Donner Avenue between Sixth and Seventh Streets was constructed in 1900. During the strikes of 1919, the tracks were patrolled for fear of bombing. (Greater Monessen Historical Society.)*

It was progress of sorts, but far from what the workers wanted. The famous Mother Jones, a symbol of labor resistance during the early decades of the nineteenth century, was scheduled to speak to the Monessen workers. She traveled all over the labor fields and could be found supporting coal miners, steelworkers, autoworkers, and railroaders. She was white-haired and around 89 years old. Once in Homestead, she said, "We are to see whether Pennsylvania belongs to Kaiser Gary or Uncle Sam." Kaiser Gary, of course, meaning Judge Gary of U.S. Steel. Since the ordinance against meetings was still in effect in Monessen, the workers had been walking to Charleroi every Tuesday, Friday, and Sunday to meet. By mid-October, the coal mines were also on strike. The federal government called in 2,500 troops to keep the calm in southwestern Pennsylvania and northern West Virginia. Six companies of infantry and machine gunners from Camp Zachary Taylor, Kentucky, were camped along the river in Monessen. Fearful that trains would be bombed, the P&LE tracks were patrolled regularly.

When, by the end of November, there was no progress in the steel strike, an outside agency was asked to come in. Steel refused to negotiate. The strikers had just voted to stay out. So, the Interchurch World Movement (IWM) was selected. They set up their own plan to end the strike:

> 1906 To mediate in behalf of all the steelworkers, both those still on strike and those who had gone back to work.
> 1907 The purpose of mediation should be to establish a new deal in the steel industry rather than merely end the strike.
> 1908 The ending of the strike should be arranged solely with a view to giving the new deal the best possible chance.

Judge Gary whipped out that old red herring fallacy and accused the IWM of being infiltrated by communists. He refused to even address the issue of the steel strike until the issue of IWM's communistic tendencies was resolved. He ended his lengthy speech on December 5 by once again stating the myth that the men at work were content and those who were still on strike were "nothing but a group of red radicals whom we don't want anyhow."

The strike dragged on. Since Gary insisted that there was no issue, there were no discussions. On January 8, 1920, the strike was called off by the National Committee. They had gained little, but their men were starving. The union had no strike money to help them. Despite the end of the strike, public opinion would not allow the issues the men were fighting for to go away. Judge Gary continued to insist that the men preferred the long 12-hour days and 7-day shifts, but the United States government pushed the issues. Page's mill was the first in Monessen to see the light. In March of 1920, they began the 8-hour day. In June of 1923, the rest of the industry announced it would begin to move toward an 8-hour day as well. It would take nearly a decade to get there.

What did come out of the strike was a sense of power for the men. Unionism was "just around the corner," a corner that would be turned in the 1930s. The turmoil also gave the immigrants a sense of their own power. When the decade ended, Monessen no longer voted Republican. The "Foreigners" had flexed their muscles and won. The Americanization of the immigrant, not to mention Monessen, was on its way. They had turned on the Republicans and the "Americans," their sheer numbers eventually dominating thought and politics in the town.

*The Monessen office of Pittsburgh Steel Company at Twelfth Street was a masterpiece of Georgian-style architecture. This picture was taken in 1915, prior to the addition of a third floor and the bridge linking the building to the machine shop next door. (Raymond Johnson II/Greater Monessen Historical Society.)*

# 4. Living Life in America

Diversity defined Monessen in the 1920s. In this decade, there were 4,645 students enrolled in Monessen schools, representing 27 different nationalities, primarily Americans, Italians, Slavs, and Carpatho-Rusyns. The smallest groups were comprised of two Bohemians, three Mexicans, two Serbians, and five Austrians. Almost all of the ethnic groups had their own church where services were conducted in German, Italian, Slavic, Greek, Syrian, and a host of other languages and liturgies. This diversity is Monessen's greatest gift and heritage. When Monessen received its radio station, WMEJ, on February 21, 1927, the ethnic groups had an airwave voice. Eventually, ethnic music and stories bounced along the air waves and into the homes. But the 1920s were about more than diversity. The United States began reaching for its destiny and so did the nation's women. Monessen women won the right to vote along with the rest of the country and like the rest, cut their hair, raised their hems, lit their cigarettes, and went dancing.

The boom was still on for Pittsburgh Steel. Oil had been discovered in Texas and Oklahoma (not to mention in Titusville, Pennsylvania) and seamless tubing was in big demand. More than one wildcatter saw his fortune gush into black gold through Pittsburgh Steel pipes. At the urging of the Pittsburgh Urban League, the mill hired an African-American social worker to mediate between the mills and its black workers. They did no such thing for the immigrants, who had their own unresolved issues. They did, however, become the first of the independent steel mills, or "little steel," to begin the 8-hour day. It happened in 1923 and affected the three steel-making departments: the blast furnace, open hearth, and blooming mills.

Page's major commodity was fence. In the beginning, the fence was all hand-woven, but as time went by, it was manufactured on looms. Page got the idea for his fence while still a soldier for the Union Army. He thought there ought to be a better way to enclose property than the wooden fencing that required so much maintenance. Weaving steel was a new idea at the time and Page is the man who made it work. The first fencing manufactured by Page's can still be seen in some of the backyards of Monessen. It looked like 6-inch squares of wire. By the time the Monessen mills were in full swing, Page's had customers all over the world,

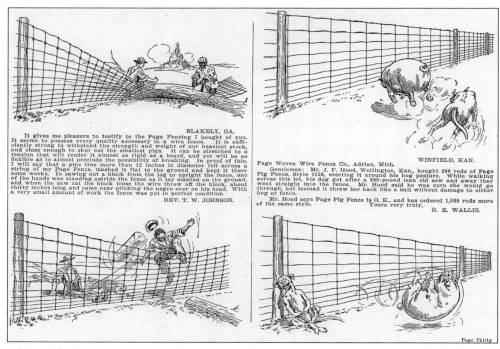

BLAKELY, GA.

It gives me pleasure to testify to the Page Fencing I bought of you. It seems to possess every quality necessary in a wire fence. It is sufficiently strong to withstand the strength and weight of our heaviest stock, and close enough to shut out the smallest pigs. It can be stretched to a tension that will render it almost as rigid as a board, and yet will be so flexible as to almost preclude the possibility of breaking. In proof of this, I will say that a pine tree more than 12 inches in diameter fell across a string of my Page Fence, mashed it flat to the ground and kept it there some weeks. In sawing out a block from the log to upright the fence, one of the hands was standing astride the fence as it lay mashed on the ground, and when the saw cut the block loose the wire threw off the block, about thirty inches long, and came near pitching the negro over on his head. With a very small amount of work the fence was put in perfect condition.

REV. T. W. JOHNSON.

WINFIELD, KAN.

Page Woven Wire Fence Co., Adrian, Mich.

Gentlemen: Mr. J. F. Hood, Wellington, Kan., bought 200 rods of Page Pig Fence, Style 1028, erecting it around his hog pasture. While walking across this lot, his dog got after a 300-pound lean old sow and away they went straight into the fence. Mr. Hood said he was sure she would go through, but instead it threw her back like a ball without damage to either hog or fence.

Mr. Hood says Page Pig Fence is O. K., and has ordered 1,000 rods more of the same style.

Yours very truly,

R. E. WALLIS.

Page Thirty

*This ad for Page fence appeared in a national magazine (as well as their catalog). As seen here, Page made fence for hogs, sheep, cows, general stock, poultry, lawn, garden, cemetery, and fire escapes. Each was slightly different, requiring a different weave. (Greater Monessen Historical Society.)*

including the United States government. The government used Page fence at Yellowstone Park, the National Zoo, Central Park in New York, Bronx Park, public stations, asylums, and observatories. In Africa, Page fence was used to keep lions at bay. In India, it held tigers. In South Africa, Page fence was put in the sea to keep sharks out of the bays.

By the 1920s, the incredible diamond-patterned, chainlink fence, invented in Germany, became a Page product. It became so popular that by the 1930s, Page's own wire fence was discontinued. Page also did special wrought-iron fences and exquisite ornamental work on a special order basis. That fence can also be seen throughout the Mon Valley, adorning the entrances to older stately homes. In 1920, Page retired and his company was sold to the American Chain Company of New York.

By 1923, there were 31 industrial plants operating in Monessen. They employed 5,572 people. One of the smaller industries was the Brown Street Clock Company owned and operated by H.R. Brown and his sons Ross, Walter, and Benjamin. Benjamin would develop the clock that would bear the family moniker and send the Monessen name around the United States. The clock was completely fabricated in the Mon Valley with parts being made at the Monessen

Foundry and at the Old Radiator Works in West Newton. The clocks were assembled in the Donora store and sold throughout the country by salesmen and catalog. A 1910 catalog issued by Swartchild and Company of Chicago tells us that the Brown Street Clock was available in five, 14-foot models. They were made of cast iron and steel with a 30-inch illuminated circular dial, featuring the name of the company and either Roman or Arabic numbers. At the base of the shaft is a plaque that reads, "Made in Monessen, Pa." One of these distinctive clocks graced the sidewalk in front of Brown's store at 532 Donner Avenue, the former site of the C.F. Blair Jewelry Store. Today, these clocks still stand, but, unfortunately, not in Monessen or Donora. Some locations are Hollidaysburg and Finleyville in Pennsylvania, Chillicothe in Ohio, and Quincy Square in Boston.

*A Brown Street clock can be found on sidewalks around the United States. One once stood in front of the Brown store at 532 Donner. The clock in this picture is located in Chillicothe, Ohio. Today, municipalities and their historical societies value them. (Lillian Duvall Kepp.)*

The biggest event in the community in this decade was when Monessen, by citizen ballot, was incorporated as a Third Class City on September 16, 1921. Monessen now occupied 650 acres and its first mayor was Carl Woodward, who served the community from 1921 to 1933. In November of 1925, the Belle Vernon–Monessen Highway was opened for traffic. Wireton, Dutchtown, and Essen would be integrated into the town in 1926 for a total of 1,300 acres. Growth had been so fast and successful that there was a housing shortage.

Many of the businesses of the 1920s were to stay in Monessen for decades: Central Pharmacy, then at Third and Schoonmaker; Kirk's Drug stores at Fourth and Donner and Sixth and Reed; Gorman's Dry Goods at 404 Donner; Monessen Plumbing and Electric Company at Sixth and Donner; Layman's at 566 Donner; Cramer's at 512 Donner; Krasik's Furniture Store at 540 Donner; Eisenberg's Department Store at Fourth and Schoonmaker; and the G.F. Wright Furniture Store. Wright's eventually became Checks Furniture Store and is now the Monessen Business Center, an incubator for new businesses. It must be noted that many of the furniture companies were also funeral parlors. In the 1920s, store owners often built their own furniture. If they built furniture, they would also construct coffins. The large collection of stores secured the money in Monessen, which greatly helped to foster the growth of the economy.

Just as the businesses were settling in for a long haul, a variety of skills arose in the neighborhoods, which created jobs and livelihoods. The 1925 Polk Directory

*Stern's Home Furniture Store at 533–535 Schoonmaker Avenue in the early part of this century is typical of storefronts of the time, as shown with cloth awnings and big window displays. (Ruth Stern Schrag.)*

*This picture shows the home of the Sugar Bowl, a candy company and restaurant run by Michael Loukas at 554 Donner Avenue, next to Peoples National Bank, now Citizens Bank. It closed during the Depression. The double doors on the far right led to the telephone exchange above the bank. (George Loukas.)*

listed 24 barbers in Monessen (one who also hand-crafted violins), 12 billiard halls, 4 bottlers (who make their own soda pop), 13 contractors, 13 Express and Drayage (hauling), 9 fruit stores (mostly Italian), and 26 restaurants. Each of the ethnic groups supported their own members, not only for convenience of language or to help them get ahead, but because they had the specialty items necessary to keep traditions alive. For example, in Finntown, the folks visited John Heikkinen barber's shop, bought their soft drinks from Jacob Kitinoja, went to Abraham Knuuttila for baked goods (or a sauna), enjoyed another sauna at J. Niukkanen, and went to I. Saxberg for tailored needs. The 32 confectioners in Monessen read like a United Nations roll call: Soliema Bartus, John Biszaha, Josephine Dujardin, Samuel Essey, Victor Glogosh, Alex Kaluves, John Lengyel, Axel Ruuti, Stanley Szczpanski, Jack Wurela, and Nell Zajac.

There were shoemakers like Dominic Persico at 681 Knox Avenue and Joe Caterino at 300 Third Street. There were midwives, who often had great folk medicine skills, like Annie Kerch, Mary Babinski, Julia Banas, and Carolina Parigi. There were music teachers like Herbert Barr, Homer Buck, R.H. Curtis, Edgar Drake, Frank Rizzuto, John Jannotta, and Eva Malm. There were piano teachers, piano tuners, stenographers, and hucksters, who brought produce to the doorstep in the neighborhoods. Candymakers opened stores downtown. From the 1920s to the 1960s, people earned a living at such work not only in Monessen, but also throughout the country in a gentler, slower time. They fed, housed, and clothed their families. They sent children to college. They made a community thrive, kept the money in town, and kept the streets full of activity.

Perhaps the most famous of the entrepreneurs in Monessen was Angelo Pallini. Pallini was a tinker. Day in and day out, he tramped the streets of Monessen and the Mon Valley ringing his bell to let the women know he was arriving. They, in turn, would dash about, gathering up their knives, scissors, umbrellas, and copper kettles to be sharpened, fixed, mended, and soldered. As he roamed western Pennsylvania, he beat out the rhythm of his steps in iambs and pentameters. Angelo Pallini, in addition to being a tinker, was a poet. He wrote of immigrants, of their fears, of their Americanization, of their eventual wisdom.

But there were other forms of entertainment in the community where people of all denominations gathered. Once a year, the caravans would come to dispense American knowledge and entertainment in the form of lectures and performances under a tent. Some were circuses, some were carnivals, but a heavily attended event was the Circuit Chautauqua. The original concept of a Chautauqua, which still exists, began in Chautauqua, New York where the Chautauqua Institution created summer programs around the lake. The Circuit Chautauqua began in 1904. It spread across the country with various agencies setting up touring groups in their area. In southwestern Pennsylvania, it was the Redpath Brockway Chautauqua out of Pittsburgh. The 1914 event was held at Page Park. The newspaper reported, "The big tents will be located right along the banks of the beautiful Monongahela river, where cool, pleasant breezes can always be had and the scenery is picturesque." Once again, the entire town was bedecked with pennants and streamers. The Friday before the lectures, an automobile booster parade, led by a band, took to the streets. The traditional program began each morning with a lecture, followed by an afternoon musical event and an evening play. During the 1914 Chautauqua, Shakespeare's *Twelfth Night* was presented.

By this time, most of the ethnic groups had their own clubs and organizations. They entertained their own people through these clubs where the young folks met, courted, and married. They even held their wedding receptions there where they were entertained by ethnic bands and ate traditional ethnic wedding foods. It was almost a law that nationalities did not mingle, not in the mills and not for entertainment. Finns married Finns, Russians married Russians, and Greeks married Greeks. In fact, up until 1950, it was a disgrace if a girl married outside her ethnic group. To the Italians, that also meant a Tuscan married a Tuscan, a Sicilian married a Sicilian, and a Piedmontese married a Piedmontese. This was emphatically true among the Rusyns. The schools brought the ethnic groups together, the clubs and churches helped to keep them apart and hold on to their identity. It gave communities like Monessen a special ambiance, one that was unique and some would say wonderful.

Most of the clubs had women's and men's organizations, choirs, marching and orchestra bands, gymnastics, and ball players. In some instances, the clubs were linked to national organizations so they would belong to local and national leagues with competitions at all levels. It was a way of life. Language lessons, music lessons, dancing lessons, and baseball playoffs, all of these were offered by the clubs. Every Saturday night, something was going on, a play, a musical event, and a dance.

The clubs served another purpose, as well. They helped the new immigrants find their way. Where should a person live? The club could help. Where should a person work? The club would know. How should a person prepare for naturalization? The club would fill out the papers and ask the questions. How could one learn to speak English? The clubs would provide. How could one teach a child to read and write the native language? The clubs handled that. If someone got sick, the club dues had set aside a portion of their income to give out in times of need, much like an insurance program.

For the African-American community, there was the National Association for the Advancement of Colored People (NAACP). Although the NAACP was founded in 1909, it did not arrive in Monessen until 1929. On September 29, 1929, the chapter in Monessen, the Westmoreland County branch, held their first meeting. The 71 members in Monessen choose Dr. Henry F. Owens, their dentist, to lead them. Their concern at the time, according to Dennis Dickerson's *Out of This Crucible* was not only "police brutality toward Monessen Blacks," but "harass[ment of] Blacks who opposed the local Republican organization." Dickerson quotes a letter from Owens to the NAACP's headquarters in Washington, D.C.: "Blacks who backed the independent candidate for the city

*A Russian reader used in Monessen churches to teach Rusyn children not only the language, but also traditions and prayers. (Carpatho Rusyn Society.)*

*Anna Olsavick (top, center) treated her workers from Olsavick's store to a day on the Olsavick family farm in Fallowfield Township. Anna is shown here holding her two daughters, Helen and Ann. (Helen Olsavick Ezerski.)*

council 'were called before the Superintendent of the Mill and told flatly that they would lose their jobs if they voted against the G.O.P.' " This had also been the case for immigrants, but they had no organ to speak on their behalf.

A result of the decade of chaos that preceded the 1920s was a devastating exodus of people from Monessen. By January of 1920, over 1,000 immigrants were on their way out of the city (4,000 total in the Pittsburgh area), and that made a big impact on the landscape. In a way, it was a contradiction, for Monessen had been named the nation's melting pot by the Pittsburgh *Sun* in 1919. The Bureau of Naturalization figures claimed Monessen made more United States citizens out of immigrants than any other city in the country.

However, the immigrant was, for the most part, fed up with all the turmoil and the lack of a decent way of life. They were fed up with life in the United States, with the promise of good wages that never came. In Europe, they were peasants, in the United States they were slaves. In Europe, as tough as life was, most of them lived in the open air. In the United States, they worked in holes in the ground and in polluted mills. Nor was the community safe. The Monessen newspapers were filled with bombings, shootings, explosions, and brawls. Men were armed with hatchets, knives, and clubs. Almost everyone carried a gun. A woman gathering berries was shot with a shotgun. The water tank in the community of McMahon was blown up, unleashing an avalanche of water on the houses below.

Some workers had been black-balled by the mills and would not work again in the industry, so they returned to the "old country." Others had sided with the mills and were fearful of repercussions from their fellow Monessenites, so they left, too. One man had left his wife and five children in his homeland before the war and went home to find them. A woman had lost her husband and son during the influenza epidemic and had no income, so she returned to her homeland. Some of the people were the so-called "Reds." They left Ellis Island on December 21, 1919 aboard the USS *Buford*, an old troop carrier now dubbed the "Soviet Ark." The book *Seeing Reds* tells us that more than one-third of the deportees were from the tri-state area: Pennsylvania, West Virginia, and Ohio. Among them was Alexander Berkman, who had tried to kill the steel and coal baron Henry Clay Frick in 1892. He had been in Western Penitentiary. The Monessen deportees were listed as coming from Greensburg where they had been tried.

The 1920s brought the emergence of Monessen's own traditions. The people were settling in, finding their footing, and establishing their territory. They had fought for their right to be in the country and now they would spread out and take root. They celebrated Easter, Christmas, christenings, weddings, and deaths just as they had done in the "old country." They kept alive and frozen in time a view of life in Europe at the turn of the century that still exists in Monessen.

Europe moved on; Monessen did not. It is part of Monessen's uniqueness. Christina Kerekes said as much to Mathew Magda in his book, *Monessen: Industrial Boomtown and Steel Community*. Her family, like many in Monessen, kept all the traditions. She says the following on the subject:

> The sadness is the holidays changed in Europe and didn't change in America. When I went back to Europe, I went to a wedding, and it was not like a wedding that my mother told. They had modernized. It surprised me very much.

Picnics were a big treat for families on Sundays. The city park would not be created until 1931 and 1932, so most people went out to local farms. Perhaps one of the reasons picnics were so popular was Prohibition. People could not drink in bars, so they went onto private property in the countryside. They called it "going to Canada." A law is only good if people obey it and people in the United States did not obey Prohibition. In some families, liquor sales were part of the family's income, and in such a depressed time, giving it up was not an option. One family in Monessen sold "hooch" to put their son through college.

Zajac Farm, where the Monessen Soccer Field stands today, was a favorite. Some of the northern Italians went to two farms in Star Junction. The Hungarians went to the Evans Farm, located where Grand Boulevard runs into Monessen Highway (Tyrol). Evans sold chickens, milk, eggs, and animals. At many of the picnics, or on most Saturdays at the Hungarian Hall on Seneca, there would be a *Saluna*, a bacon roast. The men would build a big bonfire, put a cut of smoked bacon on a special long fork, top it with paprika, and, while occasionally catching the drippings on a slice of scrumptious bread, roast it over the fire.

The Finnish Socialists, like many clubs in Monessen, would lose their big hall during the Depression. When they did, they bought a farm, which they called Osuus, near Monongahela in what is now Mingo Park. They turned it into a small colony with cabins, steam baths, and a sauna. On Juhannus, the longest day of the northern year, they would celebrate with a big bonfire. The Finnish Temperance groups went to farms, too. They would cook stews to go with the Finnish rye bread they made in specially built ovens in the backyards on Motheral Avenue.

The Russians also enjoyed a good picnic. By 1939, their favorite event was transposed to the city park where it was labeled Rusyn Day. Rusyns from all over the tri-state area would come to spend a day celebrating with folks from the old villages.

The Greeks went to a number of farms in the area. Lamb on a spit was the meal of choice and the drink was *mastika* (the forte of Chions Island), which is similar to *ouzo*. Before the days when the wonderful Kennywood Park in West Mifflin was the center for Community Picnic Days, the trolley park at Eldora was the annual holiday spot. Eldora was owned by Monessen's own Roy McShaffrey, who created the park in the 1920s. Picnics eventually turned into annual events and all of Monessen would enjoy Syrian *kibbi*, *shish kabob*, and *warna arnab* (grape leaves), Greek *gyros*, *bakalava*, and *moussaka*, Italian fried dough, sausage, and pizza, and Southern sweet potato pie.

Music, not just listening but performing, became integral to the community. Fathers, sons, and grandsons could enjoy each other's company while playing side by side in a band or orchestra. All the traditions of dancing in the 1920s and 1930s were a part of the music scene in Monessen. There was the ballroom dance, jitter-bug, waltz, polka, Charleston, Big Apple, and even the bunny hop. Marathon dance found its way onto the floors of the Italian Hall and the Armory. Some bands were not for dancing, but for listening or marching. Monessen had its share of good bands. It was listening live to the Dixionians, Frankie Barr, and a dozen or so others. The citizens were bursting with pride to listen to friends blowing horns, beating drums, or playing away on violins.

Monessen has an incredible history in music. The most famous band of all was the Louhi Band, a world-class musical group organized among the Finnish community on February 14, 1900, two years after Monessen was founded. That first band consisted of 12 men under the direction of Axel Ruuti. By 1915, under George E. Wahlstrom, the band was turned into a first-class orchestra, playing classical music in concerts at the high school, the Sixth Street Park Band Stand, and later at the city park. By this time, the band had nearly 50 members and contained a library of 1,500 compositions. They rehearsed outdoors every Sunday morning at their home at 532 South Fourth Street in the Finnish Temperance Hall. Rehearsals became social events as members of the community would gather around the band or sit on their porches and listen to the music. A single female, Ksenia Tanttari Palomaki, played in the band for many years. In 1918, they performed at the All-Nations Liberty Bond Parade in New York City. While there, they cut their first record. On the Victor Label, the first side was "Maamme Laula" and the flip was "Pois Rannoilta Suomen." In 1920, they toured Finland, giving concerts throughout the country.

Louis Koski was the conductor of the Louhi Band in the early 1930s. He was followed by Walt Wiita. The Louhi Band had a youth band and many of its players were also in the Monessen schools where they participated in various band activities. Paul Passoja was the last conductor of the Louhi Band, and his leadership took the band to new heights. In June 1940, the band performed in the Finland Day program at the Finnish Pavilion of the New York World's Fair. They gave two performances. The first was an afternoon Finland Day program at the Court of Peace where the guest conductor was Tauno Hannikainen, the conductor of the Boston Symphony. The second performance was a Bonfire Program in the evening, also at the Court of Peace. They played one of the most difficult musical pieces ever written: "Korsholima." It is believed that the Louhi Band won every competition it entered.

Giants in the ethnic music world lived and worked in the town. Ethnic bands marched, gave concerts, and even played dirges as they marched behind caskets at funerals. There were so many fine bands in Monessen that it is difficult to pay tribute to all of them. One was the Monessen Drum Corps. Another was the Monessen Fife and Drum Corps. The Pittsburgh Steel Products Company created a band mostly composed of members of the Louhi Band. The Hungarians had a band led, appropriately enough, by Frank Strauss. The Firemen's Band came

*This picture shows the Louhi Band, Monessen's "pride and joy," on tour in Europe during the 1920s. They entertained the king of Finland, met important Finnish composers, and received the royal treatment from tens of thousands of fans. (Monessen Public Library and District Center.)*

out swinging in 1921 under the direction of Frank Stevenson Sr. and won many awards. Among the leaders of the band were Ernest Morrell, Frank Strauss, Frank Rizzuto, and John Jannotta. On rehearsal day, the fire trucks would come out onto the street and the band would go inside the fire hall to play.

Monessen had an Italian band as early as 1902, when 50 men formed a brass band under Professor Vincenzo Lambiase, who was brought from New York City to lead them. It was not long before Giovanni Jannotta's band of 22 pieces appeared. The latter marched in Greensburg in new uniforms made by M. Meyers and Son of Monessen in 1908. In 1919, Frank Rizzuto's pupils gave a concert on August 24 at the NIPA Hall. In 1923, an Italian Band Association, under the leadership of the same Giovanni, now John Jannotta, gave a concert at Page Park. These Italian bands combined the traditions of the brass bands of northern Italy and the festa bands from the south.

When Jannotta was conducting the Firemen's Band, they would rehearse at the fire hall on Third Street. If you forgot your music, Jannotta would give the band a 5-minute break and write the notes for your oboe, your trumpet, or your drum. He was gifted. He wrote many pieces of music, which appear to be lost now. When he died, the band era in Monessen was over, but the men got together and put a band together to march at his funeral. They accompanied him to his grave to the music of Chopin's Funeral "March" and his own "Funeral Composition."

In 1926, Monessen's Frank Lombardo began a band called the Columbia Imps. By 1931, the name had changed twice to Lombardo's Night Club Orchestra and Frank Lombardo and his Ambassadors. When he tried to register with the Music Corporation of America, he was told there was already a Lombardo in the

*This photograph shows the Monessen Drum Corps. During parades, no less than ten Monessen bands joined the line of march. (Monessen Public Library and District Center.)*

organization, a man named Guy. Lombardo changed his name to Barr and began making history in the Mon Valley. In later years, the Frankie Barr Orchestra became the house band for the Twin Coaches. Jack LaForte and his Radio Broadcasting Orchestra was one of the bands asked to play in the first series of concerts for the new Monessen City Park in 1932. It played weekly on WJAS, the Charleroi Radio Station. For the park concert, they played such tunes as "Clementine," "St. Louis Blues," "Dark Eyes," and "Wabash Blues." Some of the vocalists were Ci Nesti, Jack Stevenson, and Jack LaForte.

In 1918, M.I. Edelman announced that he had come from Chicago to take over the Ukrainian band and the Children's Orchestra and Choir. His temporary studio was in room 16 of the Grand Hotel on Donner Avenue. He taught instrumental and vocal music "with special deep breathing." In the same year, the Croatians announced that they would start their own brass band under the leadership of Charles Behrend and P.W. Fuerston. When they bought their instruments from Elkhart, Indiana, Fuerston went to the factory to select each of the 30 pieces first-hand. When he returned with them to Monessen, not only were they displayed in the window of the Ney store for all to see, but musicians paraded through Monessen playing the new instruments.

Among the earliest bands in Monessen were the gypsy bands. They would go to the bars on payday and play music the clientele enjoyed. They came from all over, but Monessen's own gypsy band was organized by Herman Mihalich. Mihalich's band grew into a regular Croatian band. He remembered, in the book *Monessen: The Story of a Steel Town*, Serbian weddings as the best. Sometimes, they lasted for three days and there was always plenty of liquor and food. The Croatians played the tamburitzian, the heart and soul of a Croatian band. There were plenty of tamburitizian groups in southwestern Pennsylvania. The first to offer training came from Cokeburg. In Monessen, three or four of these groups would exist at the same time. Today, the singing, dancing, and music is kept alive by the Duquesne Tamburitzians of Duquesne University.

Of course, there were more bands. Monessen Slovak Band, the Monessen Polish Band, and the Monessen Hungarian Band are all mentioned as participating in parades and giving concerts. There were also ethnic radio shows. Monessen's Michael Sinchak ran a radio show called the *Slovak Radio Hour* out of WHJB in Greensburg every Sunday afternoon in the 1930s. He brought it home to the valley at WMET in the 1940s. He and his son Samuel produced a book called *Slovak Songs and Dances,* which, he writes in the foreword, he hopes will bring "before the public the wealth and beauty of our Slovak songs, to which all may also enjoy dancing."

Living at 333 Schoonmaker Avenue, Sinchak acquired international copyrights for the music to such songs as "I am Proud to be a Slovak," "Hymn of American Slovaks," "Slovaks We Are," "For Our Slovak Heritage," "Plough Plough," "Even Though I'm a Mzyo's Daughter," and "The Gypsy Died." He was very active in civic and ethnic life not only in Monessen and the Mon Valley, but nationally and internationally. He was the national vice president of the Slovak League in America, which was the voice of the Slavic immigrants. He worked to assist

*The Chuck Carlo Band performed for Michael Sinchak's Slovak Radio Hour in the 1930s. From left to right are (front row) Michael Gramatikos, Charles Kozik, Larry Evancho, Michael Sinchak, Andrew Buchko, Carl Chelen, George Lesko, and Charles Evancho; (back row) unidentified, Mildred Check Marsden, Margaret Check Belak, Marian Sinchak Moneos, and unidentified. (Teresa Sinchak.)*

immigrants with naturalization and took groups on pilgrimages to Europe to the shrines of Fatima and Lourdes. He was also involved with the Pittsburgh Agreement, a document created in 1918 with the hopes of bringing independence to Slovakia. With that in mind, he traveled to Czechoslovakia.

Two elements make the bands and their music most impressive: the number of people in Monessen that enjoyed learning, playing, and listening to music, as well as all of the conductors who were able to make a living at being bandmasters. Most of the musicians held jobs in the mills, so they did not earn their living playing in the ethnic bands, but they supported the bands by taking lessons and paying for them. Their children and wives took lessons, too. Monessen knew how to read and play music. The question remains, however: What has happened to the music? It would be terrific to sit outdoors on a Sunday morning and listen to friends and neighbors making music once again.

It is time to speak of the resilient Monessen women. The "Americans" often worked side-by-side with their husbands in the stores in town and often had maids, preferably Finnish women, to help them in their homes. While H. Dallas

McCabe ran a good bit of the town, his sister Bertha seems to have had her own businesses. They lived at 660 McKee, but Bertha owned property around Fourteenth Street and kept a small book where she tracked the buying and selling of her stocks and bonds. As a member of the Evening Women's Club, she and her fellow club members presented educational programs about foreign lands, never calling upon the immigrants in their own community to tell them about their lives in the old country.

The immigrant women had a lifestyle far different from the "Americans." Few spoke English and if it were not for their children, who picked English up on the streets and in school, they would have trouble dealing with the wider community. Many women were in arranged marriages. It was nothing to see a young girl wedded to an old man because she had citizenship and he needed a way to come to the United States. The community would arrange these marriages. Women had big families. They often birthed at home with, if they were lucky, midwives. They also kept boarders, a daunting task.

Regardless of their standing, suffrage belonged to all the women of Monessen and they took to the streets to get it. In 1920, women won the vote in the United States. This modern attempt to win rights for women began in Washington, D.C. on March 3, 1913, when a Woman's Suffrage Parade was held (1848 marked the true beginning). The movement reached Monessen on Saturday, May 2, 1914, when a march through the downtown streets was followed by a rally at the corner

*Here are the working women of early Monessen: the quality control ladies of the Tin Mill, all 68 of them. They were mostly the daughters of Finnish and Rusyn immigrants. They worked in the mill from its beginning in 1898. (Carpatho Rusyn Society.)*

of Fourth and Donner at the former City Building. Led by the Louhi Band, asked to play because the women had already won their battle for the ballot in Finland, a full program of entertainment and speeches took place in front of 1,500 people. There were singing groups, like the Afro-American quartet, speeches by local candidates, who promised to support suffrage, and a bake sale to raise money for the group. Literature on women's rights was distributed and the Declaration of the Principles of the Woman's Suffrage Party was read. The ladies decorated the town in yellow jonquils, the suffrage flower, while homes, stores, and buildings around the town were decorated with yellow bunting and pennants, the suffrage color. By May 15, the Monessen group, led by Ray Motz, was meeting in Webster to start a movement there. The 1914 attempt was defeated in Congress, but the movement continued. It would have a long road to victory.

Even after the amendment was passed, getting to actually vote was not an easy matter. It appears that women were property. If their husbands were immigrants, they could not vote even if the right was theirs. If a woman was born in the

*Fashionable Linden elementary school teachers pose in 1923. From left to right are (front row) Rebecca Grove, fourth grade; Mildred Craig, first grade; Helen Jones, fourth grade; A. Zella Butler, fifth grade; and Virginia Lear, substitute; (back row) Margaret Bolig, second grade; Anna Currie, principal; Ida Gray, third grade; Charlotte Swan, third grade; and Ruth Beckman, fifth grade. (Monessen Public Library and District Center.)*

United States, but her husband was not, she was still out of luck. On the other hand, if a man was a citizen, he could vote regardless of his status. This strange circumstance affected 40,000 women in western Pennsylvania who registered, but could not vote. Another reason they could not vote was if their husbands had been classified as "enemy aliens" in the 1910s. That affected about 14,000 regional women. Voting had become a complicated issue and the barriers turned many women away from the polls, never to vote again. Women had a long way to go, creating yet another Monessen division.

This decade also saw threats to the fragile freedoms that the United States provided. The politics of the 1920s gave rise to right extremists. The Ku Klux Klan had grown strong in the United States in the 1920s and arrived in the Mon Valley around 1921. By 1924, the Klan had over 125,000 members in western Pennsylvania. They had Klavern, or clubs, in many western Pennsylvania towns, including Monessen. Their strongest inroads in the entire state were in Fayette County where the Frick Coal Company saw "a homemade illegal union-wrecking machine" and supported them. They actually conducted their cross burnings under the protection of the Frick police. The Klan was everywhere. They marched in Carnegie and Glendale, but not in Monessen. The local newspapers said very little about the organization. In one banner headline, incredibly without a story, the *Daily Independent* stated, "Night Raiders Active Again." But the book *Out of This Crucible* maintains the following:

> The Klan became active in the steel town of Monessen where scores of Southern Blacks came to work at the Pittsburgh Steel Company. Crosses were frequently burned. This activity lasted into the 1930s when at least once a month Klansmen ignited their blazing symbol of White supremacy.

Oral tradition says members would meet at night around a certain tombstone (now gone) at the entrance to Grandview Cemetery and perform their rituals or they would burn crosses on the Luce Farm.

The Klan was against alcohol, gambling, blacks, Catholics, and Jews. In Monessen, most of the immigrants were not only Catholic, but liked to drink and gamble. The book *The Ku Klux Klan in Pennsylvania* states, "The Klan's real appeal was to the group of Americans who were opposed to cultural change and to those reactionaries who wished to bring back the good old days before the so-called 'new immigration.' " They had to be the worse elements of Monessen's "American" community. They were strong far right extremists. Churches found their congregations not only infiltrated, but sometimes over-powered by the Klan. This type of conflict was strong in Charleroi, Johnstown, Scottdale, Connellsville, and Crafton, but there is no mention in the literature of the existence of such conflicts in Monessen.

In other communities, the KKK tried to gain power by trying to control politics. In fact, they were so strong in some areas of the United States that their candidate nearly won the Democratic ticket for President in 1924 and they felt sure they could put their own man in the White House in 1928. In some places, the KKK succeeded placing judges and district attorneys in local power and senators and congressmen in national power. At least one candidate for city government in Monessen in the 1920s was Klan-supported. The book *The Ku Klux Klan in Pennsylvania* reports "We had to stop one person who traveled around in behalf of H____ of Monessen. We had to tell H____ to speak for himself. The other fellow was terrible." Monessen was not prime to be victimized by the KKK. It had too many of the very people the Klan was trying to eliminate. In the brief period of Monessen's existence, freedom was sorely tested, but the town did not fall to anarchists, Reds, or the KKK. Monessen politics would fall to a different master in another decade.

*Few jobs were open to women through the decades; beauty shop workers, telephone operators, and clerks, like Margaret Ferencz seen in this photograph of G.C. Murphy's 5 and 10, were the norm. Murphy's dominated the 500 block of Donner Avenue for many decades. (Vincentine Cecelia.)*

# 5. Finding Power, Rejecting Republicanism

It was a time for meatless meatballs and no-apple apple pie. Hobos rode the rails. The Dust Bowl decimated the South. The Okies headed for California. Hoovervilles emerged on the American landscape. Unemployement rose to 12 million people. It was the Depression, and in Monessen, as tough as it was, life went on. In 1929, the Kiwanis Benefit Entertainment for the Underprivileged Child was a musical at the Star Theatre entitled *Brother Can You Spare a Dime?* It vied with *The Terror*, the first "talkie" to appear at the Star. Growing tired of having high school books hauled out for the public every evening, the Woman's Club donated 650 books and got Monessen's first public library up and running in 1936 on the second floor of the Barker Building at Sixth and Donner. The new Charleroi-Monessen Hospital opened in Lock Four with a big ox roast and parade. The little theater group called the Monessen Civic Theatre presented their play *He and She*. The Monessen City Park was created out of farm land donated by the Manown family. To access it, Seneca, now Parente, Boulevard was dug out. The vocational building was built on land that was once the Luce Farm. The firemen had a big convention with truck races, water battles, and a Mummer's parade; 2,700 of their colleagues from across the state came to participate and camp at the Luce Farm.

Someone in Monessen, despite the poverty, had to buy the new game *Monopoly* and the schools were getting a brand-new reader about two kids named Dick and Jane. In January of 1934, hundreds of people flocked to a house at 977 Donner where "the image of a dead sister appeared on the curtain in the dining room." In more light-hearted matters, the big bands came to the New Italian Hall on Schoonmaker. Benny Goodman and Tommy Dorsey beat out their rhythms and the Monessen folks skipped up to the third floor and danced the night away. If a man danced well enough to impress the bands, he could earn a pair of black patent leather slippers as the best dancer in town.

Industrial news, however, was gloomy. Pittsburgh Steel's profits fell from $4.5 million to $1.6 million, and the company would go into the red for the next five years as it fell off the New York Stock Exchange. According to an internal report,

*The Tin Mill ad in the* Daily Independent *in 1933 invited the town to celebrate its birthday. The mill entertained and fed the community at its own expense.* (Valley Independent.*)*

between 1930 and 1935, Pittsburgh Steel received fewer and fewer orders as the country began to tumble into the Depression. Soon, it was operating in the red. To cut costs, the company cut back maintenance 75 percent, closed its Glassport plant in 1931, deactivated the Pittsburgh Steel Products Company to absorb it into the parent company, stopped work on a new tube mill, and began to lose its credit standing.

The labor story in Monessen went from crisis to crisis, but none was worse than what was happening at the Tin Mill, now known as Carnegie Steel. It was on the verge of closing. In the summer of 1932, the workers, on their own, signed a petition to voluntarily reduce their wages so that they all could continue to work a full schedule, an action that came after the entire mill had shut down for a few weeks. In 1933, the mill had to shut down for 2.5 months for lack of contracts. But, regardless of the times and the tension, on its 36th birthday in May of 1934, the Tin Mill held a big party and everyone came. It started early in the morning and went on all day long with such events as a parade, drills, speeches, concerts, vaudeville acts, dancing, and boxing. In the evening, the *Daily Independent* reported, "Dancing for the colored folks will start at 8 o'clock and they will have full rights to the pavilion until 9:30 when the other guests will take over the pavilion. Music for the dancing will be furnished by Frank Lombardo and his Ambassadors."

By 1937, despite the celebration, the Tin Mill went out of business. The *Daily Independent*, still a company newspaper, still a Republican voice, failed the

Monessen public. On November 18, 1937, the headlines blared: "Carnegie Steel Not to Close Down." Two weeks later, the mill closed. Four weeks later, the machinery was moved to the Irvin Works in Dravosburg and the Monessen plant closed forever, shocking the community.

The Tin Mill had been an important part of Monessen's infrastructure. By 1929, it had employed 1,700 people, including 68 permanent women employees in the assorting department (today called quality control). It had put Monessen on the map, not only as the largest tin manufacturer in the country, but by changing the way that tin had been made for decades. The Monessen System, as it was called, revolutionized tin making. For such a plant to be on its knees was unimaginable.

No new industry came into the city to take the mill's place. Tin cans for beans, carrots, and peas would have to be made elsewhere. No new industry arrived to keep the people in the city. No new industry came to diversify the city's business and industrial base. The Finns, who made up the majority of workers in the mill, took the biggest hit of all and, with no promise of work to come, began to leave. Of the 1,600 that once lived in Finntown, only about 200 would remain. The population of the city would never again reach the 20,899 mark of 1936.

Not everything was bad news in industry. In July of 1931, just when things were getting really tough, the Page Steel and Wire Company got a big contract: to supply the wire and cable for the Golden Gate Bridge at San Francisco (not the Oakland Bay Bridge as was previously thought). The contract would bring $6.5 million into the mill, filling the pockets of its workers and helping to generate income in the stores of Monessen and the Mon Valley. It saved Page's plant and probably saved Monessen. Not only was the contract important financially, it added prestige to Page's, to Monessen, and to the workers who would do the hands-on job. The Golden Gate is one of the most famous bridges in the world. At the time of its construction, it was the longest suspension bridge ever assembled. The contract called for 25,000 tons of main cable and suspender ropes. It would require additions to the plant and increased employment. At a time when bread lines were forming and soup kitchens were opening, Monessen would reap the dividends and survive.

One of the early victims of the Depression was the Monessen Municipal Airport. It was a grassy strip of flat bottom where Hoss's and Gabriel's now exist. Small propeller planes would take off in the direction of Allen's Crossroads, Finley Road, and Belle Vernon and land by flying low over Rehoboth Church. The young boys in religious services had a hard time concentrating as they listened to the buzzing of the engines as they flew overhead. The pilots who frequented the airport were barnstormers and stunt men who loved to fly low over the valley communities. They would give sightseeing tours and offered daredevil flying and parachute jumps. In fact, for awhile, the airport held the world record for the most parachute jumps in a single day, doing it in marathon fashion. A person would jump, land, run to the next plane where a new parachute would be waiting, and repeat the process all over again. On that day, people from all over the country came to participate. In these early days of flying, when the profession was a bit of a sport accessible to everyone, the name of a city was painted on community rooftops in big white letters so pilots would know where they were. That was true in Monessen, too.

It was at the Monessen Municipal Airport that an early wingless airplane was designed. It was a big deal at the time and on the day it was to be tested, men from the military came to see how it worked. They weren't the only ones; thousands of valley citizens joined the curious. The plane was wheeled out from the Finley Farm where it had been assembled and brought to the airport. Unfortunately, the designers could not get it off the ground. Despite the activity, in 1932, during the height of the Depression, the municipality could not meet its bills. J.W. Daugherty, one of the owners of the land, petitioned the city council to pay the 10 months of arrears rent and surrender the rights to the property. He intended to convert it back to a farm. City Council conceded that it was a losing enterprise and could not hold its own.

The people of Monessen staggered under the weight of the Depression. Once again, they were tightening their belts in the land of plenty. It seems no decade was free of the struggle to win the rights the United States promised. Silk Stocking Row, the folks with the most money, had the most to lose and they did. Some of the grand houses went up for sale. Parlor maids and upstairs maids lost their jobs. The Depression was the great leveler. Shire's Department Store across the street from the Twelfth Street Gate of Pittsburgh Steel offered items on tick. On payday, the proprietor would walk across the street to the mill and get his money directly from the company. It was like a company store in the coal patch towns that surrounded Monessen.

Men who had labored for 12 hours a day for years and had put their money in the banks in the hopes of opening their own businesses lost small fortunes, some as high as $15,000. Those who had already built that dream restaurant or that long-awaited bakery closed the doors, turned the keys over to the banks, and headed back to the mills to start all over again. People would line up for hours and for blocks in rain, snow, or sunshine to get a bag of flour or a bit of sugar. There was never enough to go around. Some folks left the bread lines empty handed.

Heat for winter was an expense most families could no longer afford. Trying to find the money to pay the taxes and mortgages for their homes was tough enough. Families began foraging for fuel. Coal, as we have seen, was very abundant in Monessen. People would walk the tracks to pick up bits of coal that had fallen off the coal trains that were heading for the mills. One family on Shawnee Avenue had a coal mine in their backyard and, even before the Depression, they would send their daughter into the cave to gather coal for their furnace. Now everyone was doing it.

Scavenging for coal became a big problem. Some men began hauling truckloads of coal from closed mines and hillsides. Finally, the Progress Land Company, who owned the former Luce Farm, had to put a stop to it. One afternoon, they found 200 men, women, and children, digging for coal. They let them keep what they had, some with truckloads, but sent them on their way.

*Folks gathered at the Monessen Airport for a "look-see" of a biplane and a demonstration of fancy flying. All valley residents enjoyed the small airport, and it was always crowded. (Robert Cook.)*

Each spring during the Depression, the city and the mills turned over fallow land to the people, and by 1933, 3,500 gardens were under cultivation, in addition to the gardens already growing in backyards. Packets of seed for beans, cabbage, and other staples were also provided, but one can be sure that the Monessen folks had a few seeds of their own. The Italians grew tomatoes, which they introduced to the United States from Italy. The eastern Europeans grew *kohlrabi*, which surely they introduced. Despite the gardens, some people were hungry. Soup kitchens were established in some of the churches. At the Averof Restaurant on Schoonmaker you could get a bowl of soup with oyster crackers for 5¢. One young man would order a bowl of soup and fill it with crackers. He probably used 5¢ worth of crackers with his soup. The owner knew it was his only meal in the day and let him do it.

In 1932, the Bonus Army marched on Washington, D.C. to protest that the veterans of World War I had not received their promised bonuses. A contingency of that army arrived in Monessen on June 5, and 34 Monessen men and some of their families departed for Washington. Despite the fact that the *Daily Independent* had an editorial against the march on June 15, 1932, claiming it was designed by politicians, about 500 Monessenites gathered to see them off and to collect a few funds to help them with gasoline and food. The bureaucrats in Washington, D.C. let them gather for awhile in the public spaces, then they called in the very army in which they had served to kick them out. By July 26, 22 men, women, and children from Monessen remained with the army. On August 1, it was announced that Gertrude Mann, the daughter of Cecil Mann of Monessen, had died of malnutrition. Yet, the marchers stayed. The Depression was horrific. Anyone who lived through it never forgot it.

At last, the laws governing alcohol were changed. There was no choice; the people refused to obey them and the cost of trying to keep the public "under the law" was staggering. In Monessen, the police were just as busy as everywhere else. In 1930, a speakeasy on Marguerite Street came under attack. The owners would not go quietly and a battle took place where a man, his wife, son, and two patrons were hauled to jail. In one of the funnier incidents, a Belle Vernon man, known as the biggest bootlegger in the valley, was caught at his still in Mt. Pleasant. When the agents were bringing him down in an elevator, it got stuck between floors. He told them, "I know how to fix this," and they let him climb out. He climbed and climbed and, exiting the shaft, took off, leaving the police in the elevator.

Police reports for the year before showed that 146 drunk and disorderly counts led the list of 1,382 overall arrests. Gambling, with 141, was next. (It might be interesting to note there were also 3 arrests for fortune telling, 10 for begging, 23 dog bites, 22 wife beaters, 5 cows running at large, and 1 murder.) The ban had created a whole underworld of crime that infiltrated into all areas of the country.

In 1933, Franklin Delano Roosevelt offered the people a New Deal. This was in the days when newspaper editorials took strong stands. In a two-day front-page editorial, the *Daily Independent* took the concept of Social Security to task:

> The New Deal's Social Security Act offers the working man nothing that he cannot do for himself with any existing reputable life insurance company. If he wants to save for his old age, he can do so without having his government reach into his pay envelope for a tax to be turned over to another government bureau manned by incompetent political leeches, who don't care so much for the worker's "social security" as for their own political security.

*Learning to cook was quite a chore during the Depression, as this Monessen High School cooking class can probably attest. Students used Ritz crackers as a substitute for apples. One thing that was plentiful in Monessen, thanks to the many gardens, was vegetables, which formed a major part of ethnic diets. This class graduated in 1933. (From the estate of Lena Poletini Falbo.)*

It fell on deaf ears, while the President's fireside chats did not. Roosevelt was giving the people what they wanted to hear.

The last hold-outs of Republican Monessen shifted their allegiance to the party that was willing to help them. The people defied the bosses in the mills who often had controlled their vote. They ignored the editorials in the two Monessen newspapers, both "American"-owned and Republican in content. Because of the sheer numbers of African Americans and immigrants, Monessen became a Democratic town. The average guy had found his power at last. The promise of the United States was within the grasp of the worker.

It wasn't Social Security alone that made Democrats out of immigrants. One of the first things Roosevelt pushed through during his administration was putting the people to work in government projects. In 1934, Westmoreland County had 12,032 men working for the Civil Works Administration. Monessen alone contributed 906 of them, the largest amount in the county. The Works Project Administration (WPA) put Monessen men to work making improvements in the community. Between 1934 and 1936, a number of projects were begun that would change Monessen's face.

One of the first projects was the Vocational School, now the Elementary Center. It was constructed on the land that was once the John W. Luce Farm. This project put 191 Monessen men to work. Beside it rose the football stadium, designed by Monessen architects Mario and Raymond Celli, sons of Italian immigrants. This project employed 301 Monessen men. It is still one of the most outstanding high school sport's stadiums in Pennsylvania. Sewers were installed throughout the city. Steps were built at Tenth and Sixth Street. (The heavy metal chains that ran from post to post at the entrance to the Sixth Street steps were donated by the city to the World War II war drive.) The Ninth Street Park came about through the assistance of 48 men, who worked for 9 months to build it. The park received a stone retaining wall around part of its perimeter and concrete bleachers along the third base line. It was the centerpiece for intra-city athletics for decades. In the 1950s, the city's softball league played there and one could hear the crack of the bat from blocks away.

Sports helped Monessen through the Depression. Make no mistake, Monessen, like all of southwestern Pennsylvania was, is, and will forever be a sports town. The main fields for sports in Monessen at the time were Ninth Street Park and Page Park. Page Park was located next to the Page plant. One took the tunnel on Tube Street under the railroad tracks. If a person was going to work, he or she turned right; if going to an event at the field, a person turned left and walked between right field and the railroad tracks to the bleachers beside the river. Home plate was at the river. The kids in town had a better way, especially during exhibition games when the cost of admission was 10¢. Beside Tube Street was the Monessen Laundry, which had a sewage tunnel nearby. Kids would climb into the tunnel and follow it under the railroad tracks directly into the field.

It was not the best of fields. One froze in cold weather as the damp wind blew in off the river. The field was never grassy. There was a particularly bad patch of dirt, probably ashes or clay, in the infield. When asked about Page Park, Monessenites all responded, "It was muddy!" But Page Park saw glory, too. Five thousand people streamed into Monessen to see Jack Dempsey when he officiated a boxing slate at Page Park in June of 1934. Monessen High School played its games there. Josh Gibson, as we shall see, hit the longest ball of his fabulous career at Page Park.

There were a number of leagues in operation during the 1930s. One was the Mid–Atlantic League Class D Baseball. It was represented in Monessen by the Monessen Cardinals, a farm team for the Saint Louis Cardinals. Another was the Pennsylvania State Association Minor League, which reemerged in 1934 with six teams, including Charleroi, Jeannette, Greensburg, McKeesport, and Monessen. The Monessen Indians had such Monessen greats as Joseph Cherocci, Mooney Kachmarik, and George Manko. Out-of-town players were housed at the Grand Hotel during the season. There was also a team called the Monessen Reds, which was the only desegregated team in town, maybe in all of baseball at that time. This team broke two taboos: color and gender. There were two African-American players and two women, sisters, on the team. Monessen, at that time, would continue to have segregated teams.

One of the most outstanding teams in Monessen history was the black Pittsburgh Steel team of 1919, which took the city league championship that year. A number of steel companies had established African-American teams, including Homestead. It was the beginning, although the history is much more complicated, of such famous teams as the Homestead Grays and the Pittsburgh Crawfords that would play regularly at Page Field exhibition games. Legends like Josh Gibson, who some say was the greatest baseball player, and Satchel Page, who eventually made his way into professional baseball after Jackie Robinson broke the color barrier, often played at Page Park in exhibition games against Monessen teams. One of Josh Gibson's many legacies happened at Page Park. He hit a home run that was so far out of the ballpark that Mayor Gold stopped the game and insisted it be measured. Oral history claims it was hit a distance of 512 feet. Although sports writers claim a hit in Yankee Stadium was further than the Monessen ball, the town is in all the record books. In his autobiography, Josh Gibson claims the Monessen hit was his longest.

More than one person stepped through the batting box at Page Field and into stardom with major league baseball teams. Tom "Old Reliable" Henrich became an outfielder for the New York Yankees in the days of Keller and DiMaggio. Henrich began his long and glorious career with the Monessen Indians at Page Field in 1934. He came back to Monessen in 1956 to claim his first professional baseball contract, completing his collection and illustrating his rise "from the Monessen Indians to the New York Yankees."

In the spring of 1930, the Industrial Baseball League, comprising six teams, was formed with teams from Pittsburgh Steel, Page Steel and Wire, Firemen, Businessmen, Foundry, and Fabric-Products. Among the managers was Freddie

Feldman, a longtime Monessen enthusiast who contributed much to the community. Thomas Preston, another noteworthy Monessenite, was the president of the league. That same year, the Polish National Alliance (PNA) League was also playing at Page Field. Monessen played against Charleroi, Donora, California, Bentleyville, and Arnold City. The winners of the local leagues would go on to the regional and national games each season. There was also a Playground Baseball League. In 1931, it operated on an elimination tournament schedule and played at Ninth Street Park and the Wireton Diamond. This team was sponsored by the city's recreation department. The Playground teams included the Warriors, Swedish Sheiks, Troubadours, and Belvederes. The fast-pitch softball league, too, had a big following and was very competitive.

The kids in Monessen loved to play ball. They played in the neighborhoods before the Pony and Midget leagues got organized. The kids would get up on Saturday morning and walk around town looking for a game. There were dozens of lots like the Dennis Avenue's Star Diamond or the downtown lot where the last Manos Theater would one day stand. They were called the sockey leagues because they made their baseballs out of socks. They also made their bats from a

*Arguably the greatest basketball team in Monessen history, this 1930 team made a mark on sports in Monessen for decades to come. In the front row, "Boots" Salotti (far left) became a longtime referee in football, basketball, and soccer; Frank Janosik (second from left) became a championship MHS basketball coach; and Rab Currie (third from left) became the longtime Charleroi High School football coach. (Monessen Public Library and District Center.)*

*These men participated in the Monessen Olympics in 1922. From left to right are (front row) L. Poplosky, M. Mahusky, Pete Mahopsky, Morgan Paul, Angelo Gallupo, and Nick Young; (middle row) M. Gallupo, Tony Veschio, Ray Canova, George Swade, Chester Howski, George Mayernik, and J. Bogdan; (back row) Price, George Sennita, William Hiskey, Paul Swade, Bill Kelley, John Eberhardt, Dave Canova, and Pete Mullen. (Susanna Swade.)*

good sumac tree branch. These very gangs would raid gardens, soap car windows, and organize snowball battles with other teams during the winter.

In April of 1930, the Pittsburgh Press announced a Marble Tournament. Monessen boys went wild and 1,500 signed up to compete. They worked their way to city champion through the different wards of the town. The championship of western Pennsylvania would take place in Pittsburgh and the national tournament was to be held in Ocean City, Maryland. That same year, a model airplane meet was held at Monessen Municipal Airport.

There is another sport that dominated life in Monessen: gymnastics. There were a host of teams in the community and they not only sponsored national events in the clubs and halls of Monessen, they often brought home the first class prizes. The Rusyn Gymnastic Sokol was organized by the Greek Catholic Union and the Slovak Gymnastic Union Sokol Assembly Number 47 on October 4, 1903. The Turn Verein, more commonly called the Turners, organized in Monessen in 1905 and laid the foundation for their building on January 17, 1909. Each group had children's, women's, and men's teams.

Of all the sports in Monessen, the two most exotic games were *morra* and *bocce*, both Italian in origin. *Morra* could be played anywhere. All that was needed were two men, each with a hand, five fingers, and a big voice. Simultaneously they would throw their hands at each other putting up a number of fingers and shouting out a guess at the combined total. The closest to the number got the points and the drinks. It was a great game for a rainy afternoon. *Bocce* needed clear weather. Each spring, the two *bocce* courts in Monessen, one at the NIPA Hall and the other at the Italian Hall, were graded, sanded, and packed down to a smoothness better than glass. A small *pallino*, a tiny iron ball, would be thrown down the court. One team would try to get as close to it as possible with their remaining balls, while the other team would try to knock the enemy balls out of contention. The neighborhoods would swell with noise as time and again balls were rocked, socked, and smashed.

The biggest industrial news stories of the 1930s were the strike, the Wagner Act, and unionization. These events changed the country, giving the average person a dignity denied to them for centuries and proving that the American way *was* the way. If persistent, if willing to endure hardship, if willing to fight for the right to have the freedoms promised, the people would prevail. In 1933, the National Industrial Recovery Act (NIRA) passed after a tremendous struggle. That act gave the workers the right to have a union and for that union to bargain on their behalf. If there were any Republican hold-outs among the workers of Monessen, this decision would push them into the waiting arms of the Democrats. The coal miners were the first to win the battle for unionhood, but it was not easy; it was bloody, ugly, and often fatal. Men and their families were thrown out of coal patch houses and often went to live in the beehive coke ovens. Some fled to Monessen to family members, who, as poor as they were, took them in. Steel struggled on.

In order to outwit the NIRA and keep control of the situation, U.S. Steel decided that if the workers had to have a union, the company would organize, run, and control it. Soon "Little Steel" (Pittsburgh Steel and independent mills like it) followed. In Monessen, Pittsburgh Steel introduced its own company union, the ERP, in 1933. However, in 1935, the National Labor Relations Act (NLRB), sponsored by Senator Robert Wagner of New York, was passed. It became known as the Wagner Act and it put a stop to company unions. Steel was going through another struggle and Monessen would be at the heart of it.

Actually, two struggles were going on: the fight to have a union and the battle over which union would run the steel industry. Once again, confusion reigned in Monessen. First, the companies challenged the Wagner Act. Pittsburgh Steel claimed that its Monessen facility did not maintain interstate commerce; thus, it was immune to the Wagner Act. In a grand ordeal, lasting for more than a year, the company went to court to find a loophole in the Wagner Act. Nevertheless, Pittsburgh Steel lost because a worker at the P&LE railroad in Monessen had enough courage to step forward and say that raw materials were shipped to the mills in Monessen from out-of-state via the railroad, proving that Pittsburgh Steel did indeed conduct interstate commerce. The battle continued to the Supreme Court and was argued with other cases as *NLRB* v. *Jones & Laughlin Steel Company*.

Make no mistake, the Wagner Act was a historic Supreme Court decision. The *Daily Independent* called it a "historic broadening of the constitution." The assenting opinion was written by Supreme Court Justice Hughes, who wrote that the Wagner Act is "a legal scheme to protect commerce from injury resulting from the denial by employers of the rights of employees to organize" and from "the refusal of employers to accept the procedures of collective bargaining as a fundamental right." The Hughes Opinion, as it was called, further declared the following: "The Congressional authority to protect interstate commerce from the burdens and obstructions is not limited to transactions which can be deemed to be an essential part of the flow of interstate or foreign commerce."

While the Wagner Act was being debated, Pittsburgh Steel tried to keep the union out of its Monessen mills, but it lost again. The company appealed that decision as well. The court in Philadelphia prolonged the battle by giving Pittsburgh Steel a stay in order to study the situation. Therefore, planned elections for union representatives could not be held in Monessen. When the workers at Page's tried to introduce a union they called the Honest Deal Lodge, the company destroyed it in short order. In the meantime, the mills began giving concessions to the workers in the hopes that the men would vote to keep the in-house union. There was no great influx of company spies as in the strike of 1919, nor could the company resort to misinformation and intimidation. After the horror of 1919, laws had been passed to protect the workers, but some incidents still occurred in the valley. Judge Michael A. Musmanno spoke at a rally at a Donora roller skating rink in 1937. He often told the following story about that day:

> I spoke at that Donora rally. Much to my great surprise and happiness, this meeting was held inside a roller skating rink. Some 300 to 400 men were in the hall when I began to speak. Suddenly in the middle of my speech, the floor caved in and many in the audience fell with it. It was ascertained later that company spies had sawed supports holding up the floor.

The people were still divided. The "Americans," with their companies, businesses, and newspapers, were against the strike and wanted the men to go back to work; the "Foreigners" and the "Coloreds" wanted to gain the financial success and security they felt they deserved. Pittsburgh Steel upped the ante. In June of 1936, it began offering paid vacations. The pot was enriched in November with a 10-percent wage increase. In other words, a common laborer who earned 47¢ an hour would get 52.5¢. Since the battle was still raging, yet another increase was announced in March of 1937: now a common laborer would earn 10¢ more an hour, increasing the rate of pay to 62.5¢ per hour. A week later, the stakes were raised again. The railway employees of Pittsburgh Steel were offered sickness and accident benefit insurance. In other words, the company was willing to give its workers what they were asking for, but without an independent union. The mill announced a $5-a-day, 40-hour work week the following week. The pressure was on. It was what the workers had been fighting for since the 1882 Homestead Strike. Over 80 percent of Monessen's Pittsburgh Steel employees responded to the bait by voting for the company union. That meant Monessen would be a non-union shop. If the vote stood, it would not have a legitimate union, but a company controlled one instead.

*Welcoming black workers into the unions was a contributing factor to unionization. Page's Local 1391 in 1941 consisted of Joe Simon, Mr. Smith, John Czelen (Union president) Elmer Page, and Alvin Lucas Sr. (IdaBelle Minnie.)*

While the mills were trying to entice the workers into a different type of bondage, John L. Lewis was trying to gain control of the steel unions. He already controlled the miners, who had fought and won their own bloody battles for unionization. He brought his own style of warfare to the mills by forming the Steel Workers Organizing Committee (SWOC) in June of 1936. Lewis threw his own brand of propaganda at the workers in order to elect his union men for the mills. As the mills were offering paid vacations, Lewis was saying, "The President Wants You to Join the Union." He sent that message to the southwestern Pennsylvania workers by creating nine districts of which Monessen was one. Of course, he neglected to mention to the workers just which president wanted them to join the unions.

Monessen's SWOC representative was John Mayo, who also served Donora, Charleroi, and Allenport. Mayo began calling meetings in Monessen for the creation of the union. One of the first meetings was held at the Polish National Alliance on Knox Avenue on September 4. Very few workers showed up, a far cry from the thousands that had marched in the streets in 1919. The newspaper and the companies went wild. They accused the organizers of being outsiders, but Mayo stood strong, saying, "We are not discouraged . . . We are going to stay . . . We are not outsiders."

It would take awhile, but the meeting attendance would grow. Perhaps the wisest thing Lewis did was welcome African-American workers into SWOC, the first time African Americans received such an offer. They flocked to the union. The National Negro Congress (NNC) worked in support of the union by meeting with and urging blacks throughout the area to support SWOC. In Monessen, the first vice president of Local 1229 was an African American.

Where locally the men appeared to be bending, nationally the men held on. Unionization was worth the hold out. When it appeared that the offers would fail, the company began talking to the SWOC, accepting it as the worker's choice and as a union. It was a major victory. Delay after delay occurred. SWOC called the men out on strike in mid-May of 1937. It was only then that the company realized the union was here to stay. They recognized SWOC on May 15, 1937. Throughout the industry, the SWOC became the union of choice. It changed its name to the United Steel Workers of America (USWA) sometime later. In Monessen, it was Page's that first signed a union contract with its men. As part of a Pittsburgh-based steel mill, it was part of what the industry called "big steel." (Pittsburgh Steel was "little steel.") Those larger mills signed a historic contract agreement that provided a "$5 minimum daily wage, a 40-hour week, paid vacations, seniority rights and grievance procedures."

By midnight on Christmas Eve, 1937, the people of Monessen had a great deal to celebrate. The community had made it through the toughest decades of the century without too much damage. As families gathered around the Christmas Eve table, they gave blessings. It was good to be alive, to be American, to have enough food on the table, to have a job that paid well and offered some security. One can argue that this was the "greatest generation." Ordinary people, mostly peasants from Europe whose ancestors had withstood oppression for centuries, had stood their ground and gave mankind its greatest gift: the right to live in dignity and determine one's own destiny. This is the generation that fulfilled America's promise. They finally understood that freedom was a gift that had to be monitored or someone would surely sieze the power.

*The Vagabonds of Short Street pitched in to buy this Oldsmobile with their hard-earned cash. They took it everywhere, even to Kennywood, which took all day. (Daniel "Boots" Salotti.)*

# 6. SCANDAL, WAR, AND MORE SCANDAL

The most devestating event in the 1940s was World War II. The most fascinating events were the two political campaigns that book-ended it. In 1941, the ill-fated Opera House burned to the ground without ever rising to its potential. Monessen founded an art club. In 1946, there was another major fire; the Monessen Senior High School burned in one of the worse fires in the city's history. In the same year, one of the most ambitious plans since the founding of the town happened: the development of the Monessen Park Plan. The community continued to change. Pittsburgh Steel had an open house and 1,500 people came to see how steel was made. A brand-new, state-of-the-art, art deco theater called the Manos opened on Donner between Third and Fourth Streets. The former Manos, a block higher up the street, became the Grand.

Industrially, the war would save Monessen once again, especially Pittsburgh Steel. As the threat of war intensified, the United States government contracts began to come in and the mill began to recover from the devastating decade of the 1930s. The federal government built Blast Furnace Number 3, the Jane, to accompany the two existing furnaces built in 1912. A by-product coke and chemical plant began operating in July of 1942. By the end of the war, it had produced 2,103,357 tons of coke, enough to fill 35,056 railroad cars making a train 267 miles long.

The mill retooled for war: welded wire fabric for Air Force airfields, 1,040 miles of Pittsburgh safety highway guard for ship landing mats and truck tracks, 19,000 tons of bullet core wire for 780,000,000 bullets, 8-way steel wire pallets for shipping and storing items like rockets, and 26,500,000 square yards of welded wire camouflage netting, enough to cover the city of Monessen four times over. Pittsburgh Steel also gave up its private Electra Junior airplane, which now sits in Australia's Museum of Flight at Nowra in New South Wales.

Page's also thrived on government contracts. During the war, the plant manufactured torpedo net wire, stainless electrodes for armor plate for ships and tanks, Signal Corps field conductor wire, aircraft control cable wire, and specialty items. Throughout the 1940s, Page's tested aluminum and steel until they were the first on the market with a hot dip aluminum on wire for the utility company. It was called the ACSR wire and the company licensed it to Bethlehem Steel in the 1950s. In 1947, Page's erected two new buildings for its chainlink fence. Where Pittsburgh Steel raised a wooden billboard in front of its main office on Twelfth Street, announcing its participation in the war, Page's had a permanent bronze plaque erected at the entrance to the plant. (The community had erected yet a third on Donner Avenue near the Armory.) Pittsburgh Steel inaugurated the *Keystone Magazine* to enhance its image in the community and sent copies to its employees overseas. Page's had a magazine called *The Page Patter*, which served the same type of audience. By this time, the company was producing aluminizing fence.

Industries in Monessen had trouble filling the vacant jobs and manpower was at a premium. Pittsburgh Steel's recruiters traveled south and lured African Americans to Monessen. It wasn't enough. Women came out of the home en masse and went into the factories across the United States. Women did everything from making candles to making parts for war vehicles, working in every conceivable industry. Over 6 million women took over men's jobs. In 1944, the average woman's salary was $31.21 a week. Men in the factories made $54.65 a week for the same jobs. The worse jobs and the poorest pay went to African-American women, if they got hired at all.

In 1948, Rockwell, now the owners of Monessen Foundry, intended to double their factory's output in Monessen. They purchased a lot across Monongahela Street from their buildings. It was formerly the site of the Monessen Brewery. They intended to hire additional men, but they became embroiled in a political conflict and, as we shall soon see, left Monessen. Nothing came in to replace Rockwell.

Before the war, the 1941 political scene was catapulted into a full-blown scandal when Carey L. Schuck printed a series of articles in the *Monessen News-*

*Landing strip wire manufactured in Monessen by Pittsburgh Steel is being rolled out to form an airport landing strip in the sand by American soldiers overseas. (Raymond Johnson II/Greater Monessen Historical Society.)*

*C.L. Schuck, the owner of the* Monessen News-Call, *kept Monessen on the straight and narrow, as he saw it, for nearly 40 years, while he served as owner and editor of his newspaper.* (News.*)*

*Call* maintaining that the community was being ruled by criminals. Schuck had been a farm boy from Ohio who came to Monessen and bought the *News* in 1902. He was a man on a mission and his newspaper voiced his attitudes. He was a conservative Republican and so was his newspaper. He was involved in every aspect of Monessen's development.

Schuck called the manipulation of politics by the rackets the "Third Party" of Westmoreland County. He claimed that the exploitation went back as far as 25 years and that the biggest problem was in the district attorney's office. He argued that neither of the mayoral candidates, Joe Lescanac or Daniel Reamer, would take a stand on the issue. He offered as proof the enormous amounts of money spent by certain candidates and begged that the election be sent to the grand jury. Schuck asked, "Why are numerous bawdy houses, gambling dens, numbers rackets and scores of other nefarious vice activities permitted to continue unmolested in Monessen, when even children of grade school age know about them?" In the end, he did not win. The majority in Monessen voted Democratic. They had not forgotten what the Republicans had done to them.

In a show of political correctness that would manifest itself again and again over the next decades, the houses of prostitution in Monessen were raided in October of 1941, just before the elections. As the Monessen raid was taking place, a similar raid was taking place in New Kensington at the other end of the county. In Monessen, 5 women were arrested as proprietors of the houses and 20 girls as inmates. The 7 men (customers) were released on a small fine. In the house at 1338 Schoonmaker, police also found slot machines and added this to the list of charges against the madam of all the houses. The *News-Call* ended its article with, "According to reports, the houses resumed operations within a few hours after the raids."

When the *News-Call*'s backed candidates lost the election, Schuck continued his attack on the winners. He wrote an open letter to the new district attorney, calling on him to clean up politics and clear out the rackets in Westmoreland County and Monessen. Oral tradition claims that Schuck's motives may not have been as noble as one supposed and that during the time of the articles, instead of printing the usual 1,500-copy print run of his paper, he printed 20,000 papers to be distributed all over Westmoreland County. In turn, if the candidates he backed were elected, he was to get the county printing jobs. Both parties would do anything to gain power. If Schuck was right, then the rackets did what the KKK could not do in the 1920s: they had infiltrated politics for their own gain. The majority in Monessen stood against religious and racial discrimination, but they did not mind gambling and prostitution.

C.L. Schuck would not be the man to win this battle. He died in March of 1946. His obituary states that he "pioneered in the development of nearly every major highway entering the City." One of his biggest visions was a highway linking the Pennsylvania Super Highway in New Stanton, the first of its kind in the United States, to the Mon Valley and points west. It was a long-term dream and eventually came true with the development of Interstate 70.

Bouquet Flats, a deteriorated split-level housing unit with dirt floors cascading over the hillside from Morgan Avenue, was to be torn down. The mines under the city were beginning to elicit concern. For some time, a fire had been slowly burning under Wilson Avenue; it had reached dangerous proportions and had to be put out. The Monessen Brewery was slated for demolition. Charleroi-Monessen Hospital received a new wing. The P&LE terminal received a facelift and became a bus terminal as well as a train station, managed by Andrew Janosik and serving the Blue Ridge, West Side, Doernte, and Hilltop bus lines.

As for the streets, the community was still riding on Belgium block, a brick made for paving streets, and the main streets had streetcar tracks running down the middle. Congestion was a major problem downtown, the streets were too narrow, parking was not being observed correctly, and something had to be done. To fund the project, the city planned to float a $350,000 bond. Statistics show how necessary the improvements were: 230 men worked at the Monessen Foundry, 1,000 men worked at Page's, and 6,000 men worked at Pittsburgh Steel. There were 350 retail stores in Monessen. The city had 27 miles of paved streets, 21 miles of sidewalks, and 22 miles of sewers. The area was continuing its rapid growth.

World War II burst upon Monessen in 1941 with the bombing of Pearl Harbor. On that day, December 7, 1941, you could buy a pair of slippers at Samuel's Shoe Store for 99¢, a housecoat at J.C. Penney's for $1.98, get a permanent at La Rosa Beauty Shop for $3.50, and purchase a butterscotch chiffon pie from Johnson's Restaurant for 49¢. The Star Theater was featuring *The Maltese Falcon* and the original Manos had *All that Money Can Buy*. The city has just celebrated a huge Christmas parade and was settling in for the holiday season. When folks tuned in to the radio on that Sunday morning, their world changed forever. Within a few days of the bombing, Company G of the Third Regiment of the Pennsylvania Reserved Defense Corps was fully organized and on full war alert. They arrived in Monessen and patrolled the Charleroi-Monessen Bridge and Lock Number 4. They lived at the Armory and ate at Johnson's Restaurant.

The War Price and Rationing Board Number 65-8 also sprang into action. It consisted of three men: William G. Weil as chairman, J. Karl Beery, and Dave Woodward. They met in SWOC headquarters at Eighth and Donner (CIO Hall, now Landmark Place). The unemployment office was there as well. In addition to sugar, coffee, cigarettes, and metal products, gasoline and tires were closely rationed. Monessen's quota of tires varied from month to month, but for January 1942, the community was limited to 14 passenger tires with 12 tubes and 28 truck tires with 23 tubes. Priority at inspection stations was given to emergency vehicles, doctors, nurses, ambulances, fire trucks, and police cars. People received ration books at the banks and used them to get the scarce items.

The local draft board, Board Number 10, consisted of Robert J. McKelvie, Clarence G. Murphy, and C.L. Schuck. By September of 1941, before the attack on Pearl Harbor, they had examined 482 men of whom 326 had been deemed 1-

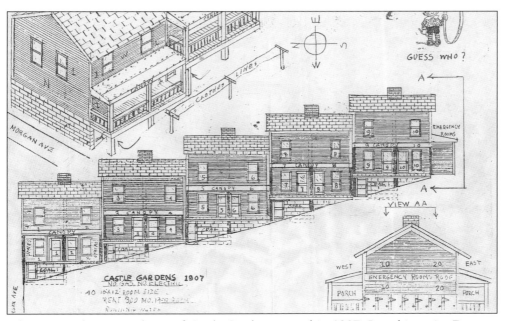

*This is an architect's rendering of Castle Gardens, erected in 1907. It and its twin, Bouquet Flats, housed many Monessen families before the structures were torn down. Both were located on Morgan Avenue, one going up to Highland, the other down to Schoonmaker. (Greater Monessen Historical Society.)*

## Monessen's "Brownout" Started Monday, Jan. 29, 1945

Beginning Monday, January 29, 1945, the Merchants' Group, C. of C. will comply with the War Production Board Order U-9 to help conserve the nation's coal shortage, and requests the full cooperation of all to adopt the beginning date as of Jan. 29th instead of the effective date Feb. 1, 1945.

Day or night, there shall be no outdoor advertising and outdoor promotional lighting.

Day or night, there shall be no outdoor display lighting except where necessary for the conduct of the business of outdoor establishments.

Day or night, there shall be no show window lighting except where necessary for interior illumination.

Day or night, there shall be no marquee lighting in excess of 60 watts for each marquee.

Day or night, there shall be no outdoor decorative and outdoor ornamental lighting.

Information on the use of directional or indentification signs, and other information may be obtained by calling the Chamber of Commerce, 945, or West Penn Power Co., 1100.

**Your Cooperation is Solicited for Monessen's "Brownout." Starting Date--Monday, January 29, 1945**

*In addition to the rationing of food and gasoline, the folks back home were asked to keep the lights dim in case of invasion. Monessen, because of its mills and its lock on the Mon, was a likely target. (Valley Independent)*

A, 103 were approved for limited service, and 53 had failed their exams. Of those numbers, 120 had already been inducted into the army from Monessen. When a registration day was called, as on February 16, 1942, the city schools were used as registration centers and the teachers manned the tables. Failure to register carried a $10,000 fine.

As during World War I and the Depression, the city and industry gave people plots of land near the city park to grow vegetables, calling them "victory gardens." Each evening after work, men would walk to their designated plot from all sections of town to till and maintain their gardens. Weekly victory garden columns ran in the paper, telling people how to keep a garden. Liberty bonds were back, too. There were over 10 drives through the war years, but not too many parades. Rallies were the ticket in the 1940s. Monessen women under the leadership of "Mrs. Republican," Elizabeth Duvall, led the county in sales. Courses were held in civil defense. Homes were blacked out from 8:30 p.m. to 5 a.m. daily. Black-outs became mandatory in 1942. In March, the *News-Call* announced that Air Raid Headquarters was at the Municipal Building with sub-stations at the Hungarian Hall, Saint Leonard School Hall, the Croatian Hall, and Pittsburgh Steel.

To keep morale high, many patriotic events were prepared. Each industrial plant had its own honor roll, while a city honor roll was dedicated in 1943. Radio stars and movie stars dropped in to sell war bonds. A Navy caravan of United

States and German weapons stopped in Monessen for two days in August of 1943. On the morning of D-Day, June 6, 1944, in the darkness before the dawn, the church bells of Monessen slowly began to peel, calling the people to prayer. One by one, residents came out of the morning mist, tracing their steps to the places of worship they had built and sustained through the years. The doors remained open all day long as worshippers left their homes and jobs to come to the silence of the houses of God.

Many of the businesses in town won minuteman flags from the Treasury Department for their sacrifices. These flags were given to firms who had 90 percent of their employees turn 10 percent of their salaries into bonds. Among the places in Monessen to fly such a flag were Pittsburgh Steel, Page's, the Monessen Foundry, and G.C. Murphy's. The biggest prize of all was the "E award" given by the army and navy for "Efficiency in handling government war contracts." Pittsburgh Steel, whose Allenport and Monessen plants were working up to 90 percent on war contracts, won the award in 1943. This War Department award was the highest civilian accommodation and the only time in western Pennsylvania that the award would be given to two plants of the same company, especially at the same time. It was a big celebration in the community. The ceremony took place on March 18, 1943, beginning in the morning at Allenport and continuing in the afternoon in Monessen. Lunch, by invitation only, was at the Elks club on Seventh Street with Johnson's Restaurant catering.

Monessen had its own National Guard unit, Company D of the 28th Division, which had come to the city from Beaver Falls in 1924. When the Japanese bombed Pearl Harbor, Company D was on maneuvers in North Carolina and expected home on December 9. On February 17, 1942, Company D became part of the federal Army. They trained at Indiantown Gap before being sent to England in 1943. From England, they went to Normandy in July of 1944, a month after D-Day. They were involved in five campaigns and returned to the United States after V-J Day. The 28th Division was given the epithet "bloody buckets" by the Germans because the Pennsylvania state insignia, a red patch in the form of a keystone, was worn on their shoulders.

The soldiers sent back letters of thanks that were printed in the *Keystone Magazine*:

> In going through Braunau, Austria, we overran an Allied Prisoner of War Camp. To my surprise two of my best friends . . . were being held at this camp.

> I am now in the Third Army, "SWEATING" it out down here in Southern Germany, near Wurzeburg. I think I have it made if I can just outlive it. Yes the war is over as far as this Theatre of Operation is concerned and I am sure "Pittsburgh Steel" had a hand in the great victory with the grand production records you have been setting.

Who knows better than we here in Burma? Without you folks back there we'd sure be in a mess here. The job back there is just as important as our jobs here. We get what we need and when we need it, thanks to you. I'd like to say "hello" to my many friends back there especially the men of Central Steam Plant.

I handle all kinds of ammunition. We are working on 155mm, 105, and 75—at present. I remember how they used to stack them up, in the old tube mill. Well, it's 3 years now for me. So I'll say thanks again and keep the good work up, and if anyone cares to write I'll try and answer.

The 28th Division went on to Japan, but most of the Monessen boys were mustered out, having completed their tour of duty. In September of 1946, the *Saturday Evening Post* had an article called "They Took the Nazis' Sunday Punch," the story of Pennsylvania's 28th Infantry Division as it went from Normandy to Germany. Part of the article details the Battle of the Bulge where the 110th Infantry Regiment, mostly southwestern Pennsylvania men, held the center of the United States line. Company D returned home to the Armory at Ninth Street and Donner, now the James Manderino Gymnasium on July 15, 1946. Not all Monessen GIs served in the 28th, however; some served in the Virginia National Guard's 116th Regiment, 29th Infantry Division ("the blue and gray"). They hit the beaches at Normandy on D-Day with a number of Mon Valley men in the first wave. Still other Monessen men were a part of the 83rd Division of the Ohio National Guard.

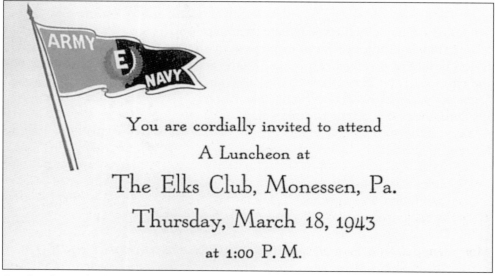

*Pittsburgh Steel celebrated its Army-Navy E award in good fashion. Monessenites coveted an invitation to the celebration and many kept the programs as souvenirs. (Greater Monessen Historical Society.)*

*Commando Kelley, Congressional Medal of Honor and Silver Star recipient, visits Pittsburgh Steel's United States Army ordinance office and poses for a picture at the honor roll in front of the main office. (Mary Grace Manderino-Sedory and Greater Monessen Historical Society.)*

Monessen boys served in the Navy, the Marines, and all other military units. Monessen played a part in this history as it did in every event that happened in the United States through the years. History did not happen to someone else in some other place in some other time. It happened here. Monessen men fought these battles. Monessen men were there when the first boats hit the Normandy beaches on D-Day. They were the heroes of the Battle of the Bulge holding back the enormous German line with the same energy and work ethic they used to build Monessen and the Mon Valley into the glory that it was. They were there in the 28th Division as the only United States army to march on the streets of Paris, France. They were in the first units to cross into Germany. They were there to liberate the death camps, to see what man can do to man when freedom and respect are lost. They turned into walking skeletons on the Battan death march. They fought those battles for the same reason that their fathers fought the companies, the unions, and the United States government. They fought for human dignity. They fought for the right of the common man. They fought for freedom.

In 1945, the *Monessen News-Call* gave some estimates of what the war had cost Monessen. The records of the Selective Service indicated that 5,200 selectees were registered for Draft Board Number 10 and 2,450 were called to active duty, not including the volunteers, which pushed the number to 3,053 on the community memorial. The memorial, on Donner between Seventh and Eighth Streets, listed 69 dead with about 200 wounded, figures that would change as time went by.

The paper said Monessen's first draftee was Staff Sergeant Albert N. Imbrescia and the first casualty was Louis C. Stephens. The war cost more than that; it cost Monessen its youth. Monessen grew old during the war and it grew weary.

The city learned another lesson about what it meant to be American and how hard it was to belong. When the war was over and the boys started coming home, the African-American population in Monessen experienced what Monessen immigrants had after World War I. Black soldiers fought for their country as Americans, but returned to a nation that still discriminated against them. There were stores in Monessen where they still could not go. There were restaurants and clubs they could not enter. Even the American Legion would not welcome them. They had to establish one of their own. They also had a Black Elks, Masons, and Eastern Star.

In 1948, Monessen celebrated its Golden Jubilee, the 50th anniversary of the town. It was a big affair with all parts of the community participating. Although it was a year-long celebration, August was the big month and the big events were kicked off with a parade on August 14. The parade was set up to be like the Tournament of Roses parade in California with 22 floats built to the specifications of the Rose parade floats. One float carried Miss Monessen Golden Jubilee, Geraldine Sappo, and her court. There were also a few bands. The line-up was completely different than that following World War I when dozens of Monessen bands welcomed home the doughboys.

Monday was called Homecoming Day and featured a registration of former Monessenites who had come home for the week, followed by a tour of the city and picnic lunch. The day continued with the opening of the Farm Frolics at the Armory and a Golden Jubilee Band Concert at the stadium where the play *Cavalcade,* a community pageant, was presented. There were also fireworks. Tuesday was Youth Day. There were tournaments in volleyball, softball, horseshoes, tennis, rifle shooting, archery, table tennis, basketball, swimming, and track and field. In the evening, there was a youth day band concert. Wednesday was Fraternal and Nationality Day, as foods and programs were at the Farm Frolic and native dances preceded the *Cavalcade* at the stadium in the evening. Thursday was Labor and Management Day. It was open house at Pittsburgh Steel, followed by a band concert at the stadium and a Jubilee Ball at the New Italian Hall. Friday was Golden Jubilee Day. The final judging of the Farm Frolic at the Armory took place where all the jams and cakes got their prizes. The Duquesne Show, a local radio show, broadcast from the stadium. The *Cavalcade* was followed by another firework display. Saturday had an auction. While all of this was going on, the Firemen had their own convention and parade, adding to the festivities.

Monessen loved a celebration almost as much as it loved a good political scandal or a heated election. The town had had its share of both. Burgess Stewart had taken the law into his own hands and refused the people the "right to assemble." Mayor Gold had had a year-long feud with the Jehovah's Witnesses. Most recently, Mayor Joseph Lescanac refused to allow council to appoint his chief of police. Headlines said that Monessen was the butt of jokes, and council meetings became heated as Lescanac fought hard to keep the right to pick his own police chief. Toward the end of the feud, Lescanac reported that he would act as police chief, while he insisted that the council-elected chief report to the city building every hour on the hour. The demand was carried out.

After the war, a group of men, who were visionary in their approach to the town's new problems, took over the administration of Monessen. Unlike the founders, they were in it for the betterment of Monessen, not to make money. Monessen had changed little in 50 years; it still had the same streets, the same buildings, the same houses. Just as the mills had to face constant upgrading, the city had to do the same if it intended to survive. The city council, with men like Dave Victoria, Joseph D'Alessio, John Molnar, and Stephen Sinchak, presented two proposals to the people: to build 300 to 500 new homes and pave all the streets in town. The houses, with preference given to veterans, would be between four and six rooms, sell between $6,000 and $10,000, and be located in the new Park Plan. One month later, it was announced that the city would receive 150 federally funded low-income homes, which would be realized in the next decade and become the Park Manor.

In 1945, another election for mayor was held. One of the candidates was a young Italian-American named Hugo J. Parente. Parente owned an insurance and travel agency in town and served the community as an alderman. The primary

*These Monessenites participated in the drama* Cavalcade *presented at the Monessen High School Stadium during the 50th anniversary of the community in 1948. (Monessen Public Library and District Center.)*

*This political cartoon appeared in the* Monessen News-Call *during the 1945 elections. It attacks the "so called" Democratic machine. (*News-Call)

was a heated contest between Parente and the incumbent mayor, Joseph Lescanac. The *Monessen News-Call* accused Parente and a few other candidates of receiving campaign contributions from county officials who, in turn, were receiving money from the racket bosses.

The newspapers had their own candidate in mind: Republican J. Karl Beery. Beery came from another longtime Monessen family. He was "American" and Republican, while Parente was "Foreign" and Democratic. Both Monessen papers began a lengthy campaign to defeat Parente in the fall and bring the Republicans back to power. Through political cartoons and front-page editorials, the battle lines were drawn. Parente was accused of pandering to the criminal element in the community and the county. The newspapers dredged up all the scandals in Monessen from prostitution to gambling to double parking in downtown. It didn't work. The vote was tight. When it was over, Parente won the battle by just 76 votes.

Once Parente was elected, one of the first items on his agenda was an order to close the red light district in Monessen, but it did not happen instantly and it did not happen without a lot of personal strife. The newspaper applauded his effort. The *News-Call* claimed that vice had "made the town infamous over a large area" and "Parente has placed the first feather in his hat as a good government mayor." However, this was not going to be an easy chore for the mayor. He had worked for the man in charge and they had a friendship.

In 1949, Parente ran again. It was a hard-fought primary with Parente's main opponent being John Spielman. Monessen was now 7 to 1 Democratic. Yet, there was no complacency in the community as 9,372 people, 90 percent of the registered voters, turned out to vote in the election. Parente won again.

Parente was becoming bigger than life. He was a born politician and had enormous charisma. The people loved him. He had opportunities to go beyond small-town politics and run for bigger offices, but he refused them. He loved being mayor and the people loved him in the role. He would walk down the street and tip his hat to the ladies. Someone could call and ask who the best doctor was for hemorrhoids and he would not only find out, but he would make the appointment and see that the person got there. The Hemorrhoid Club kept growing and was a constant joke in the community. Even the *Daily Independent*, usually putting Parente through the hoops, allowed the following:

> We have said many times that the Mayor has the ability to be a first rate executive for the City. We have felt also that he has a sincere interest in Monessen. We believe he would strengthen himself with the people, however, if he would cease to regard himself as just another cog in the machine and stood squarely on his own feet.

Perhaps that was a tough call for a politician to make with the Democratic machine so strong at mid-century. Perhaps it was a more delicate and demanding job to juggle all the possibilities, placate as many elements as possible, and keep focused on getting the job done. Parente seemed to be able to do this and he got better and better at it as years went by.

Unfortunately, coast to coast, America was becoming unglued. Monessen was not the only community facing the inroads of criminals on the political system. Organized crime appeared to be in control and something had to be done. Hugo J. Parente and his town were about to embark on a decade that would shake the city to its foundations.

# 7. As Good as It's Gonna Get

Poodle skirts and crinolines, ice cream sodas and convertibles, drive-in movies and car hops, the Dog House, Caminos, Tall Toms, what a time it was. The mills were working. The city was sprucing itself up. Families were buying homes and automobiles, exploring the mountain resorts or taking off for Atlantic City, New Jersey for fun on the beach. Ethnic clubs were swinging on Saturday nights. Americanization for the immigrants was nearly complete. In 1950, the city began to implement the 197-acre Monessen Park Plan and erected 314 Admiral and Gunnison homes. With the new expansion of the city that was to take place in 1950s, the ethnic neighborhoods were beginning to dissolve. It wasn't perfect. Despite the fact that, in 1948, the National Democratic Party introduced a civil rights plank, African Americans in Monessen were still restricted in the community. No homes in the new housing development, the Park Plan, were open for African-American families. Meanwhile, Monessen immigrants were still locking horns with "Americans" over ideologies. A new parking plaza for 122 cars was built in the center of downtown. Sadly, the city bought the P&LE station, tore it down, and created a parking lot. They would do the same to the Star Theater and the post office.

On a happier note, Monessen received a large, spacious library. A parade of 1,400 students from the Monessen Junior-Senior High School walked in line the few blocks to the new library on Donner from the old library on Fifth Street, each carrying a few books. In 1953, the foundry, now an empty hulk, was torn down to make room for a new shopping center, the second in the city (one was under construction at the Park Plan). The Monessen–Belle Vernon Civic Music Association presented their yearly theatrical programs by world-renown musicians, vocalists, and entertainers. Another mine fire burning under the city at the west end near Rostraver Township, just above Route 906, would cost a small fortune and a lot of time to put out. The fire, if left unchecked, would eventually threaten the Park Plan and Graham and Lookout Avenues.

For the steel industry, the end of the war overseas heralded a new war: 15 years of strikes by the unions. The first strike began at Pittsburgh Steel on January 20, 1946, when the workers forced the government to increase steel prices so the companies would take their salaries off of a wartime footing. Workers would strike

*This dramatic view from the sky shows Jane Blast Furnace as it looked when first completed by the United States government. The blast furnace is where iron is made. Like soup, it needs a variety of ingredients; in this instance, iron pellets, coke for fire, and limestone for flux. (Greater Monessen Historical Society.)*

again in 1949, 1952, 1956, and 1959. Where once they were less than 4 percent, in this decade, labor salaries would rise to a whopping 34 percent of the mills' budgets, second only to materials. The men, ever greedy for more, would fudge on test runs for incentive, cheating Pittsburgh Steel out of an honest wage. Yet, the men wanted more.

In 1950, the aging Pittsburgh Steel made a move to modernize and remain competitive on the market. Avery Adams was hired as president with a mandate to cut costs, balance production with finishing, diversify the product line, and expand the facility. He introduced the "Program of Progress," which increased the open hearth capacity, created a blooming-slabbing mill, relined blast furnaces, and built the hot and cold Allenport rolling mills. The sheet steel rolled in the Allenport plant would be sold to Chrysler for the manufacture of automobiles and to Westinghouse for appliances. Chrysler was so keen on using only "sweet" Monessen steel for their automobiles that they provided the $8 million the company needed for the new mills. The Avery plan would create 1,000 new jobs.

The women were gone from hands-on work in most departments of the mills. Those who remained were office workers. To get such a job, a woman would have to begin as a messenger. Messengers delivered the mail and memos to the various parts of the mill twice a day. If the bosses were satisfied and if one agreed not to marry, practically unheard of today after true civil rights were awarded to all, an office job was waiting. Of course, widows could work in the mill, too. Ladies worked as telephone operators, secretaries, and typists.

As usual, everything was not positive. In July of 1953, a mill locomotive carrying hopper cars to the Number 12 furnace in the open hearth jumped the tracks and snapped a 30-inch steam pipe. It could not have happened at a worse time; it was lunch and a number of men were seated and eating in the area. They became stuck in the debris with the steam hitting them. It took 17 hours to dig them out. "I was afraid we'd roast in the steam," a survivor told the press. Five men died.

In 1953, it was election time again. Parente, of course, would run. He had his hands full, both in the primary against his chief of police Michael Ferencz and Councilman Stephen Sinchak, and in the general election against one-time Democrat-turned-Republican Dr. Joseph D'Alessio. By this time, Parente was secretary to beleaguered Congressman Augustine Kelley, who was suing, and

This political ad was run by Michael Ferencz's committee in the 1953 election against Hugo J. Parente. (Valley Independent.)

therefore exposing, the book *U.S.A. Confidential,* which claimed that racketeers from New Kensington paid for his campaign.

Throughout the primary, the *Daily Independent* took up the *News-Call*'s attack on the corruption in Monessen, aiming directly at Parente. By May 12, a few days before the election, the paper was crying foul because it had found the dead, the moved, and the doubly registered eligible to vote. An organization called Operation Crusade took out a full-page ad pointing out the different attitudes of all the candidates of Westmoreland County and asking the people to vote for right. Parente won the primary and he won big. He swept all the precincts in the city. The rest of the county slate won, too.

In the fall elections, Parente would be pitted against D'Alessio. D'Alessio had been a longtime Democrat and a 16-year member of city council. He lost his last bid for council and claimed that Parente had a hand in that, so he became a Republican. Perhaps the thought was that Parente was winning elections not on the issues, but because he was Italian and the Italians were the majority of citizens in Monessen. If two Italians would run against each other, surely the issues would be the key.

D'Alessio came out of the box with a 15-point "I Accuse" ad that blasted Parente on a number of issues. In one of the major issues, D'Alessio held Parente responsible for Monessen losing Rockwell, formerly the Monessen Foundry, to Uniontown. He claimed it was because Rockwell now made parking meters and the city of Monessen bought parking meters from someone else. More importantly, Rockwell had purchased the old brewery site across Monongahela Street from their factory and wanted the city to give them the street property so they could link the two sites and expand their business. The city did not act on this idea.

Rockwell, in the following issue of the newspaper, said neither accusation was true. It is true that Monessen did not buy meters from a company in the community, but it had more to do with third-class cities being required by law to accept the lowest bid. Rockwell stated that it had closed its Monessen plant long before it decided to open in Uniontown. The loss of Rockwell did harm Monessen. No industry came in to replace the manufacturer, leaving the city with old buildings that they would eventually have to tear down at public expense. No one won.

Three of D'Alessio's accusations had to do with the sewage. He claimed that Parente wanted to give the contract for a new sewage system to a Pittsburgh firm and float a $1-million loan without competitive bidding. He also accused the mayor of bulging the parking and traffic flow problems in Monessen's downtown and, of course, allowing gambling and prostitution to run rampant in Monessen. Parente never answered the accusations against him. Day after day, D'Alessio pounded his points into the minds of the Monessen voters. Editorials in the newspaper reinforced his claims. The editor hacked away at the Democratic machine, calling it, "a group of opportunists whose main concern is not the public welfare, but their own selfish interests." By the end of October, the *Daily*

*Independent* claimed that if the machine won, the rackets would return in force to Monessen. None of it mattered. It was a Republican voice in a Democratic town and it didn't have a chance. When the final tally was in, Mayor Hugo J. Parente defeated Dr. Joseph D'Alessio two to one with over 80 percent of the population, a staggering number, voting.

The heated political scene of the 1950s only added to the overall festive air of the community. There were more bars and clubs in Monessen than any other type of business. Every hotel had a bar. Every club had a bar. Downtown, from one end of town to another, they dotted the landscape until they numbered over 100, including the Rainbow Gardens with its live entertainment, the Swallows at the Twelfth Street entrance to the mill, the Mill Café nearby on Schoonmaker Avenue, the Aquarium where the PNC Bank now stands on Donner Avenue, the Sugar Loaf, and the Sit n Bull in the strip mall. In the neighborhoods, there was Como's, serving thin-crusted pizza topped with American cheese; Lancas' with *galatchi* (garage keys) sandwiches, the ends of crusty bread scooped out and filled with spaghetti sauce; Jesse's, now Kopko's, with the best fish sandwiches in the world; Mihalich's; Bar 20; and a host of others.

Many bars and clubs offered entertainment and that led to a cottage industry of bands. These were not the marching bands of the 1920s and 1930s, but a host of new bands that provided dance music. In the clubs, typically, were ethnic bands playing polkas, line dances, and waltzes on accordions, violins, and exotic instruments like the oud. In the bars, bands like the Meyer's Band, operated by Ralph Meyer playing saxophone, were the ticket. They usually played at the Rainbow Garden, the Red Hanger at the former Monessen Municipal Airport location, and the old Trocadero.

One step up the ladder from the bars and clubs were the nightclubs. In Monessen, some of these clubs were world class. The biggest night club in Monessen's history was the Arch Tavern, which was owned and operated by an African American, at the corner of Clarendon Avenue and Sixth Street. The three-story, brick building, formerly owned by the Finnish Socialists, was bought by Callie Mickle and his wife, Bertha. Arch Tavern attracted Count Basie, Cab Calloway, Ella Fitzgerald, Ray Charles, Duke Ellington, and Dinah Washington. The place was more than a nightclub—it was a community center. On the ground floor was a pool hall, once used as a co-op boarding house by the Finns. On the second floor was a bar, club, and restaurant, once used as a rehearsal hall. Teenagers would go to the Bebop club off the bar and dance to the juke box music.

Diners would enjoy the wild game fare, shot by Mickle himself, in the woods around the city. It was very common to see groundhog, squirrel, opossum, and deer on the menu. The third floor of the yellow brick building was the ballroom. The young kids could skate there during the week, but on Sunday night, the big names in music would come for entertainment. Eventually, the Arch Tavern was purchased by the Fellowship Church, but later burned to the ground.

If the Arch Tavern was not the biggest nightclub in Monessen, then the Park Casino was. Located on Grand Boulevard near the Monessen Shopping Plaza, it was the hottest place in town. The club had 11 owners, including Mayor Parente. There were two levels to the Park Casino and three bars, which were always alive with activity. Like the Arch Tavern, the Park Casino was a multi-purpose facility with bowling alleys on the top floor, side rooms for card clubs and meetings, and a huge nightclub with a dance floor and long bar on the first floor. Sometimes the place was so full that people had to wait outside. When one patron left, another could enter.

One of the most successful nightclubs in the United States was the Twin Coaches, owned by Tony and Rose Calderone of Monessen. It broke all odds. It was not in the center of a great metropolitan area, but was in rural Rostraver Township, which was farm country. Yet people came from all over southwestern Pennsylvania to see the first class acts. The Twin Coaches is a Monessen success story. Rose's father bought an old club that had been made of two railroad coaches joined by a dance floor. One coach was the bar and the other was the restaurant. Eventually, the coaches disappeared, and a Rose room and, later, a Butterfly room were added. When that was complete, the facility seated 1,200 and those seats were filled every night. With acts like the Ink Spots, the Mills Brothers, Tony Bennett, the Mcguire Sisters, Dean Martin, Andy Williams, Pearl Bailey, Nat King Cole, the Supremes, and Liberace, the "Coaches" was the most important nightspot in three counties.

Everyone went to Twin Coaches: Harry Truman, John and Jackie Kennedy, and even the churches. Every church banquet and church-sponsored celebration was held at the "Coaches." The Italians would schedule their banquets when an Italian-American was singing. The Poles would hold out for Bobby Vinton, who

*The house band of the Twin Coaches was Frankie Barr and his orchestra, seen here in an earlier incarnation. Frankie is on the far right. (Monessen Public Library and District Center.)*

*The graduating class of 1927 had a reunion at Twin Coaches in 1952. Mayor Hugo J. Parente is in the fourth row, second from the right, with his arm around a friend. (Frederick Feldman.)*

sang them Polish lullabies. The whole family would go to Twin Coaches to see the shows. It even had a matinee. Every big political event was held there, too, as were the big sports banquets: Big 10, Big 33, they were all at the "Coaches." So were major African-American banquets. The October 25, 1953 testimonial dinner, honoring Bessie C. and Thomas F. Preston, brother and sister educators whom most of Monessen respected and loved, was held there. Twin Coaches was part of the fabric of life in Monessen. Sadly, in October of 1977, Twin Coaches burned to the ground, too.

The African-American community still moved to its own cadence in Monessen. They were still restricted. One lunchtime hang-out for teenagers allowed blacks in the main store, but they were served their sodas in paper cups and asked to eat their sandwiches outside. They were permitted to skate at the Piggy Wiggy Skating Rink on Wednesday only and at the Beehive in Charleroi on Monday only. The movie houses accepted their money, but they had to sit in the balcony. Even the banks in town would not give them loans. They had to go to the credit companies at higher interest rates.

African Americans had their own businesses, too. They went to Lizzy Jennings Beauty Shop; to their own grocery, Michols, at Ninth Street and McMahon; to their own doctor, Dr. Crump; and to their own dentist, Dr. Owen. They even had their own Girl Scout Troop with Pauline Crabtree, later IdaBelle Minnie, as leader. Peggy Owen, daughter of the African-American dentist, had won a seat on the high school May Queen Court in the 1940s, which was quite an accomplishment in a steel town.

In the 1950s, however, blacks still had to petition the school to get representation on the May queen ballot. There was no denying that Monessen was still a rough town and that every minority had to earn the right to be an American. The city was no different than the rest of the country in that respect, but ideas that communities came up with to resolve the problem made each region unique.

The biggest story of this decade was gambling and prostitution. As soon as the mills began to thrive along the riverfront at the beginning of the century, these two industries crept into Monessen and continued to grow as the city grew. Occasionally, there would be an item in the paper that arrests had been made, but most of the time, the two "businesses" were left alone. For example, a gambling den existed above a coffee shop at 470 Schoonmaker Avenue in 1921. In 1934, the chief of police visited several gambling places in Monessen, including one at 1576 Schoonmaker, a pool room at 117 Schoonmaker, another at 1160 Schoonmaker, and a "well-known gambling place at 455 Donner," the last of which would create quite a stir over the next few decades. A true story that circulates in Monessen surrounds a gambler winning $80,000 at the Getodo Club. He was too scared to go home with the money, so he called the police station and asked for an escort—he got one. Unfortunately, as in most blue-collar towns in the United States, these types of industries cannot be forgotten.

Most Monessenites loved to gamble and they bet on everything. Local sports were a big event, especially when rivals Monessen and Charleroi played football. From high school football and basketball to the Pitt Panthers, Penn State, the Pittsburgh Steelers, and even Notre Dame, the bets ran high. All over town and in the mills there were "numbers men," who went around to the betting places to collect the bets and pay off the winners. Almost every dairy bar in town sold numbers; it kept them alive. After all, how many cokes and potato chips could you sell?

During the 1950s, places like Mickey's Dairy Bar on Rostraver, Lefty's on Schoonmaker, and Puleo's on East Schoonmaker, were gathering places. Kids came running in looking for cho-chos, licorice popsicles, and ice cream. Mothers collected a forgotten loaf of bread or bottle of milk. It was nothing to see a kid come into the dairy bar with a slip of paper with numbers on it for his mother or for the men in the local neighborhood. No one blinked. No one got arrested for corrupting a minor. No kid was taken away from his parent. They all managed to survive, grow up, have families, and have few scars. When the numbers business was abolished by the state, the corner dairy bar disappeared in Monessen. Nothing replaced them. The money they brought into the city was taken away by the new state lottery.

Gambling was big business in Monessen. It wasn't just numbers; it was big time games and off-track betting. And it all went on right in the heart of the downtown district. Amid the dress shops, the shoe shops, and the restaurants were the doorways to the "joints." Two of the biggest joints in town were the horse betting joint on the third floor of 529 Donner Avenue and the exclusive casino on the second floor at 455 Donner Avenue. The *Daily Independent* called the latter "high-stake games for a selected clientele." The two were called the Getodo Club, one of the most notorious clubs, not only in Westmoreland County, but also in the state of Pennsylvania, and maybe on the entire eastern seaboard. The Getodo was named after the first names of its three owners. There, thousands of dollars were thrown over the card and crap tables in an hour, millions in a month, tens of millions in a year.

Along with gambling came prostitution, and the prostitutes were open for business at both ends of town. The biggest area was on Schoonmaker Avenue from Seventeenth to Twelfth Streets, the five blocks between the two gates of Pittsburgh Steel. They operated in the individual homes tucked into the edge of the cliff above Schoonmaker, specifically 1528, 1530, 1532, 1534, and 1536. They were always busy.

Monessen prostitutes did not street walk, at least not in this era. Those seeking their services had to go directly to the homes where they practiced. Even young boys, eager for a rite of passage, screwed up their courage to attempt a visit, only to be grabbed by the ear and escorted out if they were underage. On the streets, the prostitutes were well dressed and well behaved. They shopped in the stores for their clothes and shoes, went to beauty parlors, stopped at the banks, and ate in the restaurants. On a regular basis, they even reported to the city building where a few local doctors would be sure that they were without disease. In fact, one former newspaper boy fondly remembers, "They were good tippers. The paper was 3 cents and they always gave me a dime."

The Madam in Monessen married a New York "tough" whose arrival in the community is the stuff of legend and is, coincidentally, linked to the shoot-out at the P&LE station in 1918. That was the biggest scandal to ever rock the town. It began at a restaurant at 320 Schoonmaker and continued up through the middle of the business district to the train station and post office on Donner. When it was all over, there were three dead: Antonio Scardazzone (Tony Longo), Joe Bassacagti, and Antonio Bua. The last two men were allegedly from California, Pennsylvania. Longo owned several businesses in Monessen, including the small restaurant where the Monessen Public Library and District Center now stands, and he was also the king of prostitution in Monessen. The funeral for Longo was huge, with Italians turning out in numbers to pay their last respects. It appeared as if his murder would never be solved, but it was, in fact, disclosed years later.

Although some names must still be protected, the story is as follows: Tony Longo took the Madam from St. Louis when she was just 12 years old and brought her to Monessen, where he made her work as a prostitute. Surprisingly, he also fell in love with her, and so they were married. In the meantime, her brothers were searching for her and when they learned that she was in Monessen, they put a hit out on her kidnapper. The man they chose to carry out the job was the "tough" from New York, who was living in Pittsburgh at the time. The tough came to Monessen and cased the place, then hired a few men to come to town to kill Longo.

*Jack and Josephine Ross were the owners of the Mill Café. Jack is in the background of this photo facing left. His wife, Josephine, is in the center wearing the dark dress. (Greater Monessen Historical Society.)*

Longo received a note to meet someone at the P&LE train station. When he arrived, carrying two guns, there was a shoot-out, and he was shot and killed. One of the hitmen died on the spot, while a second made it as far as the post office and fell dead. A third got as far as the armory. Longo was put into an ambulance. Before the doors were closed, a man standing on the street jumped in beside him, another of the tough's thugs who was to make sure that Longo was dead. Two weeks later, the tough came to Monessen. Not only did he get the business, he also got the girl. Oral history maintains that the tough changed his name when he relocated to Monessen, since he had allegedly committed murder in New York. Together, the tough and the Madam ran the major prostitution houses in the city. Five decades later, they were still in business.

Most of Monessen did not mind the gambling and prostitution. The kids were eating. The town was safe. The mortgages were being paid. Besides, Monessen was connected, which made the chest of the blue-collar workers puff up with pride. In fact, it was so legal to gamble in Monessen that one-armed bandits were installed in the clubs in town. Of course, not every one was happy. In 1944, the *Daily Independent* wrote a front-page story on the slot machines, claiming that informants estimated 75 slot machines in the "25-odd fraternal and nationalistic organizations." This was true. The clubs could have the big bands, while keeping up with their bills and repairs and stocking their shelves with booze, since the one-arm bandits were paying the bills. The clubs split the revenue equally with the racketeers, who owned the machines, and were clearing between $20,000 to $30,000 a year. To most of the people of Monessen, this made good economic sense.

Most people dropped a nickel, a dime, or a quarter into a slot from time to time. The *Daily Independent* groaned that they were "such a popular instrument of amusement here and [have] achieved such general acceptance by people in all walks of life that, although it is plainly an illegal device, there is nothing clandestine or *sub rosa* about it, except perhaps the extent to which it is protected by law enforcement officials."

In December of 1949, just after the election, the American Legion tried to buy its own machines, thereby eliminating the split with the racketeers. No sooner were they installed than the long-complacent Monessen police raided and confiscated them. The newspaper questioned whether it was a post-election reprisal. After hitting the legion, the police went after three other clubs: the Polish Club, the Arch Tavern, and the Sons of Italy. None of these clubs bought machines of their own. One reason suggested for the raids is that the three clubs were too vocal in their protests against pressure from the Democrats to vote the ticket. The Democrats were now punishing them for not towing the line.

There were occasional raids, but the raid in 1948 was a different story. Running mostly unchecked for so many years, the gambling in Monessen had reached epidemic proportions. The casinos had grown and expanded. The gamblers came into Monessen for three- or four-day junkets and stayed in one of the nearby hotels. After the clubs closed at night, the gamblers would all go to Johnson's for

*This is the* Collier's Magazine *article that appeared in November of 1950 and turned the town upside-down. This particular article was preceded by a series of articles that appeared in the* Pittsburgh Post-Gazette. *(Greater Monessen Historical Society.)*

breakfast around 5 a.m. The gamblers would then call the shopkeepers in town, who would come down to open the upscale stores for them. In early March of 1948, the state police in the raid-to-end-all-raids raided the Getodo off-track betting establishment. The constabulary raced down Donner Avenue, screeched to a stop in front of 455, and battered down the street door with a lead-filled battering ram they called "the atomic bomb." The policemen raced up the steps, assaulting the second steel reinforced door and the third thick door to enter the gaming hall. They beat down walls to find the hidden telephones. They tore up counters, tables, and huge blackboards that showed racing results from Santa Anita, Oaklawn, Fairgrounds, Sunshine, and Tropical parks. They arrested four of the operators and betters from as far away as Pittsburgh, Glassport, Brownsville, and New Kensington. But they could not find the cash box. Oral history claims that the men had slipped nearly $1 million, packed in shoeboxes, through a hole in the floor and down two stories into the pool room in the basement.

The *Daily Independent* went wild. "The people of Monessen have had to submit once again to the humiliation of having an outside police agency come into town to do what our own police force should have done a long time ago and should be doing every day," it bellowed in an editorial. A few more people began to read and listen. Nonetheless, the very next day, the painters and carpenters were fixing up the place as if it was under renovation. In fact, the Getodo began splitting its services into the horse betting and general gambling establishment at 529 Donner and the newly refurbished, elegant, high-end gambling room at 455 Donner. When the gamblers were brought before the courts, they were fined $50 each and released. The judge, the former district attorney who had been accused of racket connections by Schuck, blasted the police and told them to stop using "Gestapo Methods" in Westmoreland County. He had gone too far.

Through a series of newspaper articles and books, the extent of the gambling and prostitution in southwestern Pennsylvania made national headlines, creating a big problem. *Collier's Magazine* exposed it all in November of 1950 in a seven-page report entitled "Something is Rotten in the State of Pennsylvania," *Collier's* named names and showed faces. The magazine maintained that one of the owners was the boss of the six-county crime syndicate. His sub capo ran the vending machines and jukebox business. Another ran the prostitution. Monessen knew all of this. It was not new. They may not have known about Club 48 in Brownsville, which had the biggest dice game in southwestern Pennsylvania, or Black Sams, a Belle Vernon gambling spot, but they knew about the Getodo.

Schuck must have been spinning in his grave. Local ministers, who had been protesting the gambling and prostitution in Monessen for years, began an intensive campaign to clean up the town. Prominent among them was the Methodist pastor Reverend Allan J. Howes. Howes was born to lead this campaign. He was an imposing figure with a distinguished voice and a gift for public speaking. He had arrived in Monessen just as the prostitution and gambling reached their peak and was appalled. Not one immigrant church joined the protest.

Monessen was not the only town in the United States that needed cleaning up and the Monessen ministers now had an important ally: Estes Kefauver, also the son of a minister. Kefauver was the head of the special Senate committee on interstate organized crime and was going after crime all over the country. The crime, of course, was gambling, which the state would eventually take over and run as lotteries in a few decades. Once again, revenue would be taken away from small towns and poured into places where the people reaped little benefit.

The attempted clean-up began. On November 9, 98 Protestant ministers from 3 counties sent telegrams to Governor James H. Duff of Pennsylvania and to Senator Kefauver demanding action on crime in southwestern Pennsylvania, especially Monessen. Harry Pore followed with another editorial lamenting the lack of enthusiasm among the people of Monessen. Attorney General Margiotti of Pennsylvania met with the ministers in Harrisburg and told them that he could do nothing unless they asked the county and city to clean up crime. If they failed to do so, then he could act. Harry Pore blasted out another editorial chastising the people to get involved. Ruth Love, a reporter from Uniontown, joined Harry Pore to address the ministers telling them names and events that had occurred in southwestern Pennsylvania. Love had lost her job as a newspaper reporter because she began attacking crime. Pore went to work again in another editorial, warning the racketeers and politicians that the public was waking up.

It was not long before the United Commission for Social Action, led by Methodist minister Reverend Allan J. Howes would rally Protestant ministers from four counties, 400-strong, to preach anti-Monessen, anti-Parente, anti-gambling, and anti-prostitution sermons to a shocked Pennsylvania on January 21, 1951. In one Sunday, Monessen returned to a divided society. This time, the "American"-Republican-Protestant-newspaper group fought the "Foreigners"-"Coloreds"-Catholic-Orthodox-Parente machine.

On the very same day, the Catholics of St. Leonard's, through a respected local priest writing in the Catholic diocesan newspaper *The Catholic Observer,* were told the following:

> Moderate gambling is not a sin and laws prohibiting it are unconstitutional. It is not forbidden by the Decalogue nor condemned in any book of the bible. Murder is a crime in every state of the Union because it is forbidden by the law of God. But gambling, which is no sin, is a crime only in some states like Pennsylvania where the unsepulchered ghosts of Jonathan Edwards and others of the blue-nosed Puritans of New England still rule.

Accusations from another source surfaced, calling the *Collier* magazine article a put up job by the Republicans.

Howes and his warriors, whose movement had now been dubbed "Operation Crusade," were insistent. Howes called for a meeting with Parente. When Parente declined, he went to the county. When the county refused, he went to the state. When the state did not respond, he went to Washington, D.C. He did not stop and he was not alone. By May of 1951, 15 states were on the warpath against crime. The pendulum was swinging to a conservative point of view. Howes continued. He passed out literature and named names, as did Ruth Love of Uniontown, who became Operation Crusade's crime buster. Throughout 1951, 1952, and 1953, Operation Crusade continued, offering no alternative to incomes lost, no way of bringing legitimate jobs to Monessen and southwestern Pennsylvania. It's strategy was to crush and burn.

In the meantime, vice in Monessen went into hiding. The Getodo Club closed both of its operations on Saturday, January 20, 1951. The house men, bookies, street numbers men, doormen, dairy bar owners, and young boys who ran messages for tips were given severance pay and told to get in touch in a month. Betting disappeared in Monessen. Slot machines were ordered out of the clubs and income plummeted. In fact, the chief of police told the merchants that they had to discontinue their merchandizing clubs, since they were a form of gambling.

Churches had to stop holding bingos. That gave them less money to give to the poor in the parish. It wasn't long before all of Westmoreland County dried up. Not a bet to be had. In fact, the State Liquor Board went after a few speakeasies in town at the same time, just to keep things agitated. More people without income. The Liquor Control Board (LCB) did not sweep into town; it crept in like the union spies in 1919 and poked around the community for a few weeks, gathering information. Then, like lightning, it struck. The LCB arrested seven persons and

*This* Daily Independent *staff covered the sometimes scandalous news in the 1950s. Harry Pore, the editor, is in the center of the back row wearing a light tie. (*Keystone Magazine.*)

*The raid on the Getodo Club was front page news for weeks in Monessen in 1948.* (Monessen Daily Independent.)

destroyed a big still at 1041 Schoonmaker. Monessen would be poorer, but it would be clean.

The charismatic Howes was antagonizing a lot of people and he was denying livelihood. People began to speak out. The CIO officials maintained that "From New Kensington to Monessen, from Jeannette to Latrobe we have been attacked by the forces of evil, by people who want to destroy the Constitution." As late as 2002, one man remembered, "The patrons were not professional gamblers, they were doctors, lawyers, men with money. The millworkers were really not wanted as they didn't have the kind of money to keep 'joints' like this open."

The local businessmen, who at first found the entire matter a bit amusing, stopped laughing when sales began to drop. The clubs never recovered from the economic crisis either. Some think the community still has not. No one thought to make a cry for legalized gambling in Pennsylvania. No industry came in to replace the x-rated industries that had been a part of Monessen since its founding. No newspaper or minister came up with a plan to make up for the lost revenue the people of the town had to endure.

In the meantime, the federal government started looking for other ways to bring the gamblers and prostitutes down. They began investigating tax records. One of the owners of the Getodo Club got into trouble over his citizenship. He claimed to be a lawful citizen and he voted in a number of elections, but the state maintained that he was not and had voted illegally. His trial was to be held just before Reverend Howes began his campaign, but was postponed because of all the publicity. Eventually, the trial moved to Erie where, in March of 1951, he was found guilty. By November, he was sentenced to 21 months in jail and a $1,000 fine. There was some talk of deporting him, but oral tradition maintains that he moved to California. More than anything else, his prison term ended the partnership of the Getodo. The prisoner was the "Do." The "Ge" went into legitimate business and left the world of gambling behind, while the "To" became the big head of the rackets in the Mon Valley and would bring gambling back to Monessen after Howes and his group were merely a memory.

As for prostitution, it never disappeared. Public opinion of the industry, however, did change. Prostitution was shut down for awhile, never to operate again on the scale that existed in the 1940s, but the girls were still around, even if they operated from different locations. Parente promised to close them down if he won the election. This did not sit very well with the owners, who were old Parente friends. When the crunch came, the story goes, the "tough" was ready to kill the mayor-elect. After all, Parente had worked for him as a bartender at one time. He had nurtured the political genius of the man. Now, he felt betrayed. A number of his men actually restrained him to prevent his killing the mayor.

As a matter of fact, the "tough" and the Madam were well liked. "Half of Third Street was baptized by them," said one person. "People were poor and they kept a lot of Italian families from starving," said another. "Not just Italians, Greeks too!" said a third. Despite the fact that the *Daily Independent*'s obituary of the "tough" stated that he left Monessen in the 1950s, the couple never left. In the 1950s, they began to winter in a home in Florida, returning to Monessen in the spring. The couple died two weeks apart in June of 1967. The *Daily Independent*'s obituary said that the tough was involved in politics in the 1950s, but mentioned nothing about prostitution. They were both buried in Ozone Park, Long Island.

If Monessen had held on a little longer, perhaps its destiny would have changed. Certainly, it was the gaming center of the valley, if not the southwestern part of the state. Off-track betting is legal now and some consider it to be very respectable. Monessen, however, does not have any off-track betting. Slot machines, although technically still illegal, can be licensed. The numbers game is legal, too. Monessen, a pioneer with great expertise among its citizens, gets none of the revenue. When Monessen ran the games, the money filtered through the town, helping to keep the community thriving. It was a semi-controlled industry with very little collateral crime. The city saw to that.

121

# 8. POOR CHOICES, BAD DECISIONS

After the whirlwind 1950s, the 1960s seem tame. Monessen still had a chance, but sadly, some of the choices made in this decade would doom Monessen's industry and quality of life. Everything was changing. *The Monessen Daily Independent* purchased the *Charleroi Mail* and, that same year, it became the *Valley Independent*. Then it bought the *Donora Herald*. In 1961, the Monessen High School Greyhound football team won the Western Pennsylvania Interscholastic Athletic League (WPIAL) championship and three of its boys would go on to play professional football. In 1962, President John Kennedy came to visit Monessen. Pittsburgh National Bank opened an office on Donner Avenue. By 1964, the quaint but overburdened post office was turned into yet another parking lot and a new, nondescript post office was erected in Westgate. In 1965, a senior citizen high-rise apartment building rose on Oneida Street where the Iowa school once stood. By 1970, the Monongahela River was full of mine acid, industrial pollution, and sewage waste. For all intents and purposes, it had become a dead river. Only scavengers like carp and catfish lived there.

Allison R. Maxwell Jr. replaced Avery Adams as president of Pittsburgh Steel in 1956. Maxwell tried to keep the company in balance, but the boom of the war era was over and plastic and aluminum were replacing steel. Workers' salaries had increased 222 percent, while productivity remained largely the same, unable to meet the demands these salaries were placing on the budget. Foreign imports were coming into the United States marketplace. The company was paying too much incentive pay due to worker manipulations.

Maxwell, while addressing the Pennsylvania Economic League, stated that 30 work stoppages at Pittsburgh Steel in the past decade nearly put the company out of competition. Maxwell initiated "Program for Profits" with four phases, mostly related to cutting back costs: reducing labor costs, reducing raw material costs, reducing steel making costs, and strengthening market positions.

In 1959, the workers went on an industry-wide, 116-day strike. In order to stop the strike, the company explained their problems to the media, but years of misrepresentation by the newspaper and the company made the people skeptical. In a desperate measure, the mill sent men to visit private homes. The men sat at kitchen tables over a cup of coffee and discussed the situation. Over 6,000

*The basic oxygen furnace occupied almost an entire city block. The building was 14 stories high. The precipitator, to the left of the building, kept the air clean and cost $2 million. (Greater Monessen Historical Society.)*

employees were visited, but it did no good. The workers voted to strike. As it had done in 1919, the company closed Pittsburgh Steel; it was a lock-out once again.

Before the strike was over, the workers agreed to fix the incentive pay at Allenport. It was a town secret that the men had cheated on the test runs at the Hot Strip Mill. When they were installed at Allenport, the company had ordered test runs not only to check the quality of the products, but to time the process. The men intentionally slowed down production in order to get more money once everything went on line. They had duped the company and enjoyed higher paychecks for a long time. The new contract ended this dishonesty.

One of the biggest achievements of the Program for Profits was the construction of the $18-million basic oxygen furnace (BOF) in 1964. (Europe had had them since 1952, Canada since around 1954 to 1955.) It would replace the open hearth furnaces originally built in 1907 and could make a heat of steel in 50 minutes. The newspaper reported on March 7, 1964, that when the first heat of steel came pouring out of the furnace, Pittsburgh Steel blew its sirens and so did Page's. The addition of the BOF made the Monessen plant "the most modern BOF plant in the world."

Despite the infusion of money and modernization, foreign imports, not to mention non-union domestic mini-mills, were hurting small specialty shops like Pittsburgh Steel. Pittsburgh Steel joined with the American Iron and Steel Institute to try to stop importation, but it was too late to save the rod, wire, and wire products divisions. They could not compete with the foreign imports on the market. Slowly, they would be phased out so that by 1972, the division would be eliminated. Jobs that had been in existence since 1900 were to disappear, but the men did not go without a fight.

American companies knew that countries like Belgium, Germany, and France were dumping rods on the United States market. The mills petitioned the courts, but they lost their claim. The Tariff Commission could not see the damage that these imports were causing to the domestic steel industry. By 1966, Pittsburgh Steel made another big decision: it closed the welded wire fabric. It was catastrophic for the community.

For Monessen, the worse decision the company officials at Pittsburgh Steel ever made was to merge with Wheeling Steel of West Virginia. It never took and the two entities were more like competitors than partners. By 1968, Monessen was a modern mill. Wheeling was not. Monessen was solvent. Wheeling was riddled with debt. Ironically, it was Pittsburgh Steel that went after Wheeling. As the merger was being discussed, the *Valley Independent* assessed the two companies as follows: Wheeling had doubled the assets of Pittsburgh. It ranked higher than Pittsburgh—tenth to sixteenth. It employed 12,500 people to Pittsburgh's 7,000.

*The Redevelopment Authority lifted shovels for a new beginning. From left to right are Joseph Dudas, James Manderino, Andrew S. Furmanchik, Mayor Thomas Dalfonso, and Emil Spadafore. (Monessen Redevelopment Authority.)*

*This was Eastgate at Seneca Boulevard in the middle of redevelopment and before some of the buildings were torn down. The only building still in existence is the structure on the right, which was the Holiday Restaurant and is now Felicia's. (Monessen Redevelopment Authority.)*

Despite making the new company the ninth largest in the nation, the merger was still a bad idea, as assessed by Historic American Buildings Survey and Historical American Engineering Record (HABS/HAER) historian Mike Workman:

> The fact of the matter was that the new company was composed of two integrated steel plants. When hard times came and downsizing was needed, it was clear that one would have to be shut down. As events unfolded in the 1970s and early 1980s, it became apparent that Pittsburgh Steel had, in fact, taken in a Trojan Horse.

That is where things stood at the end of the 1960s.

Meanwhile, the town was renewing itself. The Redevelopment Authority began two major projects in the 1960s: Eastgate and Westgate. The idea was to clean up the two main entrances to the community along Route 906 by ridding it of the neglected older buildings and replacing them with development. The first of the two projects was the Eastgate Urban Renewal Project, which covered 21.2 acres and contained 118 parcels of land that needed to be purchased, raised, and refocused. Relocating 88 families and 34 businesses took awhile. They were replaced by a new highway, as well as heavy and light commercial and industrial sites. Most of the business people in Eastgate were already in Monessen; they just moved. Businesses in the blighted area, like Mid's Restaurant where some of the

125

*Monessen's downtown streets were refurbished under the redevelopment plan: trolley tracks were removed, Belgium block was replaced by concrete, sidewalks were narrowed, and streets widened. (Monessen Redevelopment Authority.)*

best pies in Monessen were made, left town. It took until 1964 to complete the Eastgate project.

Westgate would come later with more major demolition. The beautiful Croatian club, with its dynamic protocol, would be destroyed. The car dealerships like Coccari's Garage would fall, closing forever. Thankfully, the beautiful building at the corner of Eighth and Donner, belonging to and saved by the CIO, would remain intact. Among the concepts for Westgate were the destruction of several streets and the relocation of citizens to other parts of town. This project included streets like Morgan and Highland Avenues. Morgan Avenue has become a myth in Monessen. It was a miniature melting pot in a melting pot of a city. Italian, Slavic, Greek, Syrian, and African-American citizens all lived along this street, a microcosm where no one locked their doors and everyone knew each other and got along. Kids played ball in the middle of the street. Women took walks up and down the avenue, stopping to gossip at various stoops. Teenagers hung out at Imbrogno's Dairy Bar. Men visited Feldman's Beer Garden. When someone died, everyone went to the funeral. When the street got torn down, the good folks of Morgan missed each other so much that they began having reunions.

The Seneca Hollow Project on the fringes of Eastgate was another major undertaking. Seneca, once named Wild Cat Hollow, was a potential short cut from the downtown business district to the newly developed Park Plan and the newer, high-end Seneca Heights neighborhood adjacent to the Monessen City Park. Council could not make up its mind as to the type of highway to construct at Seneca. One councilman wanted single lane concrete, another single lane asphalt, another double lane concrete and Parente wanted double lane asphalt. After the lobbying, it became apparent that the double lane concrete was going to win. Even Parente voted for it. Tony Mascetta, a councilman and some say Parente's potential protégé, asked him why he changed his mind. He replied, "You had me beat." In other words, he felt it best to back the winning vote. He would do this time and again. Some would consider it a double cross, but Parente thought it was simply good politics, believing that the winning vote should carry a big clout.

As with all the elections in the past, the 1961 election was going to be a battle royal. Lou Manderino, a bright, articulate, Harvard Law School graduate, ran against Hugo Parente. Mandarino's campaign was run by his brother Jimmy, a Michigan graduate of law. The Manderino family was a big family raised on a workman's salary, who somehow found a way to get educated and come back to work in the community. In the future, Lou would become a Supreme Court justice of Pennsylvania and Jimmy would be the Speaker of the Pennsylvania House.

Lou Manderino's 1961 platform offered Monessen two revolutionary agendas: the development of a junior college and the attraction of new industry. It was needed. Monessen had expanded in territory but not in scope. Parents did not want the hard life of the mills for their children, and, as a result, Monessen schools sent over half their graduating classes to major colleges and universities. The children stepped out into the world, and, unfortunately for Monessen and the Mon Valley, most never came back. There weren't enough jobs in Monessen for college graduates. Manderino's program would have helped stop the damaging drain.

Morris Bedoia, a Monessen man who did leave, permitted the Greater Monessen Historical Society to post the following message on their web page:

> Lou like JFK was a brilliant visionary. In the late fifties, many technical people saw changes in the wind. King steel was to be replaced with stronger, lighter and reusable materials. Old technology such as vacuum tubes were soon to be replaced by transistors which would be hundreds of times smaller and have a much longer life. Lou Manderino wanted to use city land and money to attract the future. Even my own father could not grasp these concepts. The mills were working three shifts, why change? People with vision put man on the moon. States with vision, Texas, Alabama and Florida, attracted new technologies. But the voters of Monessen blew out their torch when Lou Manderino was defeated in the sixties.

Lou Manderino lost the 1961 election by over 3,000 votes. He remained on council for many years, working with the city to get the grants needed to do the projects at hand. Then, he went on to his destiny.

Hugo J. Parente was connected. During this decade, Monessen received more federal money per capita that any other city in the nation. It must also be said that no other community in the valley had such projects in their cities at this time. Parente became a political giant in Pennsylvania and would reign over the city until his death. Monessen residents either hated or loved Parente. By looking at his record, one could see that Monessen was to receive the first code enforcement program in the state; he developed Eastgate and Westgate redevelopment programs to change the two main entrances into town; he built the first senior citizen housing in the nation; he instituted a library and district center for Monessen; and he was instrumental in creating the Mon Valley Health Center.

However, people not loyal to Parente's methods offered up the gambling and prostitution, calling him a double-crosser and accusing him of stealing ideas. One of Parente's biggest gifts was his acceptance of other people's ideas. With the power he had in western Pennsylvania, it could have easily been his way or no way. Nonetheless, it did not matter to him if the idea came from someone else; if it was a good idea, it was welcome. That alone made him a giant among men. Several people, when interviewed, remarked, "Hugo never kept an enemy." He always tried to find a way to do a favor or ask a favor or do something to negate the negative attitude. He did not close down the city's options for his own ego. He appears to have loved Monessen too much.

The health center was the last of Parente's gifts to the city of Monessen. It was a facility that crossed county lines (a first), gathered together medical services and organizations into one convenient location (another first), and brought the new technologies and innovative planning Lou Manderino was looking for. It was a long-awaited new industry in Monessen.

*The senior citizen high-rise apartment building in Westgate, built in 1964, was the second of three such senior facilities in the city. (Monessen Redevelopment Authority.)*

*The Mon Valley Health Center in Eastgate began as the Mon Valley Health and Welfare Authority in 1965. It was designed to coordinate the human services systems in the Mon Valley. To that end, the Mon Valley Health and Welfare Council, Inc. was established in 1971. The building was completed that same year. (Monessen Redevelopment Authority.)*

Parente was working on a plan for the central business district when he died. The town had been run by the second generation for some time. Many businesses begun in the early part of the century had sons and daughters in control, and those who did not would close as the first generation Monessenites, many of them immigrants, grew old and passed away.

It was at this time that African Americans also found their place in Monessen. When Martin Luther King stood at the podium in Washington, D.C. and said, "I have a dream!" Monessen was there. A bus load of Monessen's African-American citizens, organized by Harry McCraw, brought the news home to Monessen. The Civil Rights Act of 1964 and Voting Rights Act of 1965 were national laws. While in the South whites tried to stop the black vote, in the North, including Monessen, it was courted. Many political rallies were held in the Arch Tavern.

Among the Civil Rights legislation was Title VII, which created the Equal Employment Opportunity Commission. By 1968, 6.9 percent of the workforce in the Pittsburgh area was African-American. There had been little advancement of blacks in the workplace at Pittsburgh Steel and other mills in Monessen. That changed when, in 1964, college-educated Ronald Minnie was hired and became a buyer, marking the first time an African American had broken the color line at Pittsburgh Steel. *Out of This Crucible* tells us Minnie's father, Arthur, started in the nail mill in 1936 and ended his career as a janitor in the blast furnace department. Minnie, who had moved away from Monessen and was living in New York City, moved back to town at the company's expense.

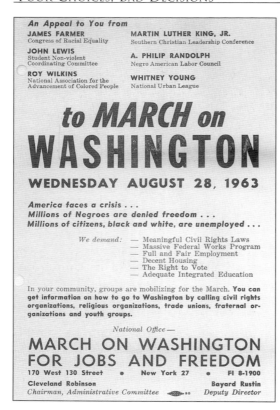

**An Appeal to You from**

**JAMES FARMER**
Congress of Racial Equality

**JOHN LEWIS**
Student Non-violent
Coordinating Committee

**ROY WILKINS**
National Association for the
Advancement of Colored People

**MARTIN LUTHER KING, JR.**
Southern Christian Leadership Conference

**A. PHILIP RANDOLPH**
Negro American Labor Council

**WHITNEY YOUNG**
National Urban League

## to *MARCH* on
# WASHINGTON

### WEDNESDAY AUGUST 28, 1963

America faces a crisis . . .
Millions of Negroes are denied freedom . . .
Millions of citizens, black and white, are unemployed . . .

*We demand:* — Meaningful Civil Rights Laws
— Massive Federal Works Program
— Full and Fair Employment
— Decent Housing
— The Right to Vote
— Adequate Integrated Education

In your community, groups are mobilizing for the March. **You can
get information on how to go to Washington by calling civil rights
organizations, religious organizations, trade unions, fraternal organizations and youth groups.**

*National Office —*

## MARCH ON WASHINGTON
## FOR JOBS AND FREEDOM

**170 West 130 Street • New York 27 • FI 8-1900**

**Cleveland Robinson**
*Chairman, Administrative Committee*

**Bayard Rustin**
*Deputy Director*

*Monessen was there when Martin Luther King said, "I have a dream" in August of 1963. (IdaBelle Minnie.)*

By 1974, local mills, including Pittsburgh Steel, signed a consent decree acknowledging their part in keeping African Americans, Hispanics, and women in poorer paying jobs, agreeing to pay them $31 million in compensation if they were hired prior to 1968. They further agreed to set "up goals and timetables for the hiring and promotion of Blacks, women, and Hispanics especially in supervisory, technical, and clerical jobs, and in management training programs."

The housing segregation was about to bend a little, too. The redevelopment was tearing down mostly poor areas and these folks needed a place to go. One agency in town sold a house to a black family on an all-white street. In order to keep the neighbors from protesting about the black family moving into a white neighborhood, the details of the sale were carried out in Cleveland, where the owners of the home lived at the time. The black family filled out the paperwork and saw the inside of their home for the first time on the day they moved in.

One of the byproducts of the demolition of portions of the city was that the wonderful buildings created by the founding fathers were falling to the wrecking ball and no one was speaking on their behalf. Monessen, not yet 100 years old, was destroying its heritage to make room for "badly needed parking lots." Undoubtedly, traffic was a problem downtown. There were too many cars and not enough places to put them. Double-parking was the norm, as were traffic jams. The solution was to widen the streets and scatter parking facilities around the community, leveling buildings to complete the project.

If Monessen had anything like a town square it was P&LE station, which faced an open grassy area on Donner Avenue, directly across the street from the Duquesne Hotel and a taxi stand. The station, comprised of brass, leather, and dark woods, a true jewel of the nineteenth century, would have to go. McShaffrey's Star Theater, too, would fall to the wrecking ball. Most of Monessen grew up there on Saturday afternoons watching the *Three Stooges*, followed by a horror flick like *The Thing* or *Creature from the Black Lagoon,* followed by a good cowboy movie featuring Roy Rogers, Hopalong Cassidy, or Gene Autry. In later years, the Keystone Players, one of several Monessen theater groups, called it home and put on such thrillers as *Dial M for Murder* and *Born Yesterday*. They filled the marquee with photos and the lights twinkled in the night once again. Just before its demise, the structure was used as a church by Saint Mary's Byzantine Catholic Church, which was awaiting the demolition and rebuilding of its church on Second Street and Reed. The Star was a true vaudeville theater and its demise diminished Monessen.

The wonderful pillared post office was tortured to death as it fell to junk. It was a neo-classic Greek, pillared, red brick and white stucco building that graced Donner between Seventh and Eighth Streets. Many care packages filled with clothing and sealed with black wax and bound for Europe were sent to the folks in the "old country" from there.

In 1972, the Louttit Building at Eighth and Donner was slated for demolition. It was the oldest brick building in Monessen. Many churches and ethnic clubs had held their first organizational meetings in its meeting room on the third floor. After a number of reprieves, the cranes finally pulled it apart in January of 1986. Across the street, the First National Bank building was next to go. Looking very similar to the bank building at Fifth and Donner, its interior was a marvel of brass cages and exotic vaults. Jefferson School on McKee Avenue was torn down in 1981. The Lincoln School would suffer the same fate.

Monessen drowned its sorrows in sports. By the 1960s, southwestern Pennsylvania was known for producing exceptional sports figures. Donora, later Ringgold, led the ranks with Stan "the Man" Musial, who played often in Monessen, plus the future "greatest quarterback to play the game," Joe Montana, who played the first game of his career against Monessen. Monessen's first pro football player, George Nicksich, according to the *Daily Independent*, was honored by the Pittsburgh Steelers and the people of Monessen on December 10, 1950. The city was wild with joy. Nicksich had been a star at Monessen High School and Saint Bonaventure University before moving on to play for the Pittsburgh Steelers. It was the first time a local sports figure had received such an honor. The plate was passed and the good folks of Monessen bought him a car.

In later years, Sam Havrilak went to the Colts in 1969 and the New Orleans Saints in 1974. Tony Benjamin played for the Seattle Seahawks and Julius Dawkins for the Buffalo Bills.

In 1961, the high school football team won the WPIAL championship with a dream team after an 11-0 season. Three of these boys would go off to the pros: Eric Crabtree played for the Denver Broncos and the Cincinnati Bengals when they were Western Division Champs; Doug Crusan played for the Miami Dolphins in three Super Bowls; and Bill Malinchak played for the Detroit Lions and the Washington Redskins. One Monessen sports enthusiast asserts that Monessen probably has more pro football players per capita than any other school district in the state.

Monessen's basketball players were amazing, too. In 1956, the Monessen High School Greyhounds beat McKeesport 53-51, scoring 6 points in the last 20 seconds of the semi-final WPIAL basketball tournament at Pitt Field House in front of nearly 5,000 fans. The team included Frank Crisi, Bob Hewitt, Ron Minnie, Bob Petty, and Wayne Cipriani. The 1988 Monessen Greyhounds basketball team won the WPIAL Class A State Championship. Richard DiBiaso graduated from Monessen and played basketball at Mansfield, coached at University of Virginia, assistant coached at Notre Dame, and became head coach at Stanford University, where he remained for eight years. In baseball, Neil Hill became a Brooklyn Dodger in 1955.

One could safely say in all the years of its existence, Monessen High School sports seldom suffered a losing season. They were mostly in the competition to the end, sometimes losing heartbreaking defeats, but keeping the fans and the proud families on the edge of their seats. It wasn't just the players—it was the coaches and the officials. Monessen had the best almost all the time. Tom Preston ran the athletic program in Monessen for many years. Freddy Feldman ran the playground activities and served as assistant on many a team from as early as the 1930s. Coach Ditty's skills reached far beyond his years as a mentor. He coached men who would become the sports leaders of the Mon Valley through several generations. Armand Niccoli, former Pittsburgh Steeler, commanded the Greyhounds for many years. Joe Gladys of Monessen probably trained more future professional football players that anyone else in the Mon Valley. He was succeeded as head coach in Monessen by Jack Scarvel who set his own impressive record. He had 10 conference championships and 14 WPIAL playoff berths. The same could be said about Frank Janosik in basketball. "Boots" Salotti and Bud Roman probably refereed more football and basketball games than any other officials in the valley. In Monessen, they were heroes, would that more of them would have come home after their careers and infused this town with the winning spirit once again.

The many and diverse city leagues still existed, but not on the scale of the 1930s. There were little league, pony league, and city league. The mills still had leagues. The businessmen had leagues. There were no professional minor league teams in the Mon Valley at all. Some adults had to find other ways to let out their sports enthusiasm. For several decades, the school programs were supported in a big way by the Monessen Booster's Club, a group of men who attended every game, regardless of the sport, filmed them, and fed the teams either before or after the games at Johnson's Restaurant. The Boosters were followed by the Mid Mon Valley

*This was the Monessen High School basketball team of the late 1950s. Five of these boys would be on the winning team that played at the Pitt Field House and thrilled fans by scoring 6 points in 20 seconds to win the game. (Monessen Public Library and District Center.)*

All Sports Hall of Fame, which, once a year, honors a sports figure for outstanding achievement. They have a small museum at the Belle Vernon Holiday Inn lobby. Someday the Mon Valley should have a big brassy shiny Sports Museum for Southwestern Pennsylvania, which would include names like Ditka and Nameth.

One other sport was big in Monessen: bowling. Bowling had been around for a long time. In the 1930s, the City Bowling League was the hot ticket with teams like Company D, Lucky Strikes, Monessen Motors, Vagabonds, Potter McCunes, and Barbers. In the 1950s, there were men at Pittsburgh Steel who broke up into such leagues as the Open Hearth League and the Blast Furnace League. The women named their teams the Monte Casino, the Bryn Mawr, the Seton Hill, the Villa Maria, and the Vassar. It is highly unlikely that any of the women went to the prestigious colleges they selected to represent.

There were a number of lanes in town to accommodate all the different leagues: Star Lanes, CIO Hall, The Hole, and the Park Casino. Teams would play each other within their leagues, then play for championships between the leagues. Although 10-pins were on the rise, the most popular bowling in Monessen was duckpins, the smaller, squatter pin. In fact, the first automatic rubber duckpin-setting machine in the world was installed at Park Casino Lanes in September of 1958. A bronze plaque commemorating the event is still on site, but the facility is now a Mon Valley Council of St. Vincent de Paul store. The games lasted all winter and then the banquets would begin: team banquets, league banquets, and city-wide banquets. Sports kept the smiles on the faces of Monessen, breaking up the differences.

# 9. THE LONG SLIDE

The 1970s and 1980s were one long agony for Monessen. The population was in decline, stores were closing, and the rehab work in the town was petering out. All of this tragedy came because the mills were self-destructing. Monessen's industry was facing a death crisis in the 1970s. There were moments of brilliance as management in the various mills tried to salvage what they could. There were moments of gut-wrenching despair as steelworkers marched through the streets of Monessen like their grandfathers had done in 1919, the anguish of lost homes, lost respect, and lost pride written on their foreheads. Foreign imports, an outclassed industry in need of updating, and a somewhat brainless government energy policy all played a part in the death of Monessen's industry and, therefore, in the near death of the community. It is almost too painful to write.

Things beyond the control of the town were happening in the United States. Midway in the decade, the Carter administration was out and the Reagan administration was in. Reganonomics was not interested in getting involved with business in such a manner and one of Reagan's first victims would be the steel industry. Under his administration, steel prices dropped 10 percent, while imports rose. The entire industry began to shrink: 509,000 men and women in steel in 1973 dwindled to 243,000 in 1983.

The giants began to tumble. J&L, the monster mill on the South Side of Pittsburgh, closed. Its famous Eliza furnace, known around the world, would be tumbled, cut to pieces, and sold for scrap. Duquesne closed. The legendary Homestead Works, where the great Carnegie mills won western Pennsylvania its number-one position in the world's steel industry over 100 years ago, unimaginatively, inconceivably, unbelievably, implausibly, impossibly was no more. Its Carrie furnaces would be shut down to stand silently like the ghosts of the past, turning to rust along the Monongahela River banks, awaiting a rebirth as a possible tourist attraction. Its 12,000-ton forging press, used for making armor plate for more than half a century, would be melted down and destroyed. This massive work of art, resembling a sculpture, would not be saved as a monument to the industrial age, as a tribute to the "Arsenal for Democracy," but melted down and reused for bullets and garbage trucks. It was humiliating. It was sacrilege. Meanwhile, Wheeling-Pittsburgh Steel (W-P) hung on.

On October 14, 1971, Parente died of cancer in his home on Silk Stocking Row. He was in his 26th year as mayor of Monessen, making him the longest serving mayor in the history of the state of Pennsylvania, for which his family received a proclamation from the legislature. In addition to being mayor, he had served in a number of government posts, including secretary to United States Representative Augustine Kelley, a member of the Workman's Compensation Board, superintendent of the House of Representatives, a member of the Local Government Commission, and coordinator of federal and state funds in Westmoreland County.

Parente is best assessed by what his opponents said about him at the time of his death. Lou Manderino, now a Supreme Court justice, told the *Valley Independent* the following:

> He was one of the greatest men in government I have ever met. He was of the people and of his time and had an unusual concern that government was there to do something for the people. I feel that my associations with Mayor Parente was instrumental in my achieving what success I have had in governmental life.

Harry Pore, the Republican editor of the *Valley Independent*, who often criticized Parente and helped lead the efforts of Operation Crusade, wrote his own views:

*Mayor Parente walked through Monessen with the Young Negro Council to find them a home, a church on Schoonmaker Avenue, which had incubated many Monessen organizations. The reward for such an effort produced one medical doctor, one lawyer, one teacher, and a funeral director. (IdaBelle Minnie.)*

Rather we prefer to think of the courage, the foresight, the shrewdness and the persistence with which mayor Parente led the fight to change an aging and blighted steel town and to give it a chance for a better future . . . The Mayor had demonstrated what can be done in local government if those who hold the power will dare to use it imaginatively against the major problems of the community. And if to boldness there be added political skill, they may be allowed to serve for long periods.

In 1973, Monessen turned 75 years old. A year-long celebration took place under the leadership of General Chairman Henry Furio. A series of banquets were held to celebrate Monessenites who had made outstanding contributions in their respective fields. Monessen at that time had four living judges: Manderino, Weiss, Hester, and Mihalich. There were three serving military generals: Mier, Kafkalas, and Burkhart. Four Monessen boys were playing pro football: Malinchak, Havrilak, Crabtree, and Crusan. Lieutenant Colonel Edward V. D'Alfonso headed the Tactical Air Force Band, which also came to play at the high school that year. Charles "Sonny" Winfield played trumpet with the band Blood, Sweat and Tears. Blanche Thebome was an opera star. George Christy and Ned Manderino were out in Hollywood, one as a writer and the other as an acting coach. Monessen paid tribute to them all. One other ex-Monessenite who was not honored, but should have been, was Dr. Christian Anfinsen, formerly of Finntown, who had won the Nobel Prize in Chemistry in 1972.

As part of the celebration, the chamber of commerce hosted a Cultural Heritage Festival, the beginning of a celebration that would last two decades and bring a great deal of pleasure to a lot of people. Probably the first such festival took

*Monessen's Cultural Heritage Festival, sponsored by the chamber of commerce, breathed new life into waning heritage pride and taught the youth of Monessen about their dance, art, and foods. (Carpatho Rusyn Society.)*

place somewhere in the early part of the century. Archives tell us that there was a Nationality Day with ethnic food and dance during the 50th anniversary. In 1972, the first of the modern festivals, Monessen Days, was held under the auspices of the chamber of commerce. Food booths were set up in the central parking lot. Churches prepared food and erected ethnic displays. A fine arts show of citizen artwork was held in the Fisher building, where a coin show was also prepared. Mellon bank sponsored a counterfeit monies exhibit. Sloga Tamburitzans, the Betsno Sloga Singing Society, the Saint Spyridon Ladies Auxiliary Choir and Singers, Saint Michael Syrian Church dancers, Saint Cajetan Church singers, Most Holy Name of Jesus singers and dancers, and the Saint Nicholas Ukrainian Church singers and dancers provided the evening entertainment. A football film series ran at the Manos Theater while a boat show was exhibited on Donner Avenue. The big event, as if this wasn't big enough, was a parade and banquet honoring the four pro football players, a kickoff of 75th anniversary activities. Meanwhile, Hurricane Agnes pelted and flooded the East Coast. That is how it began. The festival was repeated each subsequent year and had far-reaching and positive effects for the community.

The reason the Cultural Heritage Festival was so successful is that it was at the heart of what made Monessen what it is. Ethnic pride ran high at a time when ethnic traditions were fading. By 1973, the community ghettos were gone and people had shifted. Everyone spoke English, so there was no need to keep certain sections in the mills segregated. Men from all nationalities, races, and creeds worked everywhere. Monessen needed something to identify itself and the Cultural Heritage Festival was the ticket. It brought the community together to feast on sweet potato pie, kibbie, grape leaves, pasta, and other Monessen delicacies. More than that, it taught the next generation pride in their roots through dancing the "old country" dances, singing the old songs, and learning what fun it was to be involved in such events.

Over the years, the festival began to acquire too many rules, too many hard feelings, and too many obstacles. In addition, the church folks were getting older, making it easier for outside vendors to swoop in and take the chores away. Finally, a new mayor with a new idea cancelled the Cultural Heritage Festival and substituted the Festival in the Park. Where once one ethnic group alone would take in $20,000, now the outside vendors did the work and took the money away.

Monessen passed the torch to the younger generation in 1977 when James Sepesky, only 38 years old, became mayor of Monessen. He fell into the lion's den. It was not going to be easy steering Monessen through the collapse of the mills.

The saying is "the more things change, the more they stay the same." Well, the gamblers were back and 455 Donner was back in business. A single owner, supposedly with a priest as a doorman, had been operating it all through the 1960s without much notice. The den didn't have the luck of the Getodo. Perhaps all the government protection men were now gone because it was regularly raided, but was not closed until the federal government came to call. A neighbor remembers it well:

About 25 Federal Agents swept in. They let all the patrons go, but took the owner and the workers away, each in a separate car. Then a big truck with flashing lights appeared and two armed men in fatigues, Federal marshals, began removing items from the club: cards, boxes, they even took the front door.

One of the most painful events in business in Monessen in the 1970s was the closing of the famous Johnson's Restaurant. Pierce C. Johnson, the proprietor, was a fixture in Monessen. Johnson arrived in Monessen in 1907. He was 19. Together with his brother, he put up a stand with a hot plate, coffee pot, and a few china cups and saucers right next to the Star Theater. That stand quickly grew into a sandwich shop. Around 1920, Johnson bought the land and built the current building in the same location. He hustled around that restaurant saying hello to everyone to be sure they were getting the best service possible. He kept that restaurant humming and his waitresses buzzing. It was almost as old as the city itself.

Johnson's Restaurant never had a key. It doors were open 24 hours a day, every day. It closed once for an hour in the 1940s in honor of an employee's funeral. Every outing in Monessen either began at Johnson's or ended there. Almost every club in Monessen held their meetings upstairs in the banquet hall, which was known as the Cape Cod Room. The intellectual crowd held court every evening near the kitchen where they would read the free newspapers and get into heated debates about events around town. On Friday nights after the games, the Booster Club or Quarterback Club would treat the local sports team to dinner. The Saturday night crowd would stop in for breakfast around 3 or 4 a.m. and

*Ladies of the Monessen Quota Club celebrate their occupations at a Career Night meeting at Johnson Restaurant's Cape Cod Room.*

*This is Johnson's Restaurant as it appeared after remodeling in 1958. You went to Johnson's for the butterscotch rolls, the drop cake, and the omelets. You stayed for the camaraderie. It was a community treasure. (Louise Johnson Keefer.)*

bump into the Sunday morning churchgoers who would be arriving for breakfast at dawn. By Sunday afternoon, the usually unclothed tables would sparkle with crisp, white tablecloths awaiting the Sunday afternoon trade that came from all over western Pennsylvania. Johnson's was continuity in Monessen.

No business could thrive in a dying town. One by one, over the past few decades, more than 300 businesses in Monessen closed their doors. For some, the educated children simply moved on to better jobs in Monessen or, more often, out of town and out of state. There was no one to run the business that had supported the family for decades. For others, there was no business in Monessen. Malls had arrived. Monessen, like too many small towns, was mesmerized by progress and residents forgot that they should spend their money in their town to keep it thriving. Instead they dropped their hard-earned cash in South Hills, West Mifflin, and Greensburg, letting those towns prosper instead. It seemed everything was moving away, especially jobs, private ownership, and independent entrepreneurship. These were the basis for a thriving, firm-footed, free enterprise community. When they disappeared, they were replaced by franchises, chains, and conglomerates needing a larger population than what small towns could offer.

Soon, the neighborhood grocers fell. No more calling in an order in the early morning over a cup of coffee and a cigarette and having it delivered in the afternoon by a smiling, friendly face (or a grumpy, friendly face). No more charging food on tick until payday. No more homemade kolbassi or homemade cheese; now one had to buy Hormel and Kraft processed foods. In hard times, if it wasn't for the kindness of the proprietors of these small, friendly, neighborhood markets, some of Monessen's citizens would have starved.

Bigger is not better. It is never better. Half of the houses were occupied by senior citizens, and most of the widows were trying to keep ahead of the rising utility bills. The children were gone. Lower incomes and the higher cost of living forced people with nice homes to allow them to fall apart. People just closed their eyes to the unpainted porches, leaking roofs, long-neglected sidewalk weeds, and sagging retaining walls. The city looked the other way, despite the codes they were supposed to enforce.

Page's was buying rods from Wheeling-Pittsburgh's (W-P) Monessen plant. So, when Page closed, it hurt both Monessen industries. That same year, in 1972, W-P closed the finishing side of the Monessen plant, eliminating 200 jobs, the most recent in a long list of jobs lost since the 1950s. Where once 10,000 men and women were employed, now only 2,600 worked at the Monessen Plant.

The *Valley Independent* wrote an article entitled "Wheeling-Pittsburgh Steel's Monessen Plant's long agonizing death," which gave a litany of the events leading up to the 1970s. Foreign trade took over the steel industry in the United States beginning in the 1950s, forcing Pittsburgh Steel to close its fence, nail, and barbed wire production. By 1964, nearly half of the rods in the United States were imported, so in 1966, the welded-wire fabric department and number one rod mill were also closed.

Dennis J. Carney became chairman of the board of W-P Steel in 1974. Carney was a Mon Valley boy, born and bred in North Charleroi. In 1980, he would say, "Japan is in a war with us . . . It is no accident on their part. They carefully planned this war . . . to beat the hell out of the United States." The men echoed his belief. One Monessen railroad worker said, "Japan declared war on us in 1941. We beat them. We rebuilt their industry. Now they have declared war on us again with our own money."

Both were correct. The Japanese had entered the United States market in a big way; they had 26.8 percent of the domestic auto market and 14.1 percent of the domestic steel consumption. They were selling below market rate, killing the American steel industry. In addition, Japanese steel companies were not only subsidized by their government, their government worked hand-in-glove with them. That was not the case in United States—at least, not until Carney came on board.

In addition to a declining and outdated facility, Carney had another element to deal with: the Environmental Protection Agency (EPA). In 1978, Monessen had to install $28.5-million worth of air pollution controls in its plant, only one in a long litany of costs, which would eventually total $103 million for pollution control. The EPA wanted more. To say the least, this spending cost the ailing steel industry too much money.

Like Avery's Program of Progress and Maxwell's Program for Profits, Carney had a plan for the mills. Industrial diversification led the list. To that end, Carney came up with the idea of building a rail mill in Monessen. There were only two other rail mills in the country and the closest was Bethlehem Steel, which had cornered the market on rails since 1921 and was operating from an outdated plant. The second objective was to try to get the EPA to let W-P pay their environmental debts over a longer period of time. Third, Carney planned to increase the sheet price, and, lastly, he planned to get politically involved in Washington.

Carney needed money to begin his plan and he turned to the men. W-P offered preferred stock to its workers in April of 1978 and they bought $8.6-million worth. This was perhaps one of the most important things Carney did and the first of a series of moves that set W-P Steel at the vanguard of innovations, which would dominate American business for the next 30 years. Carney's creative approach to saving his industry threatened the very foundations of management-labor relations. The steel industry at large opposed his maneuvers. In fact, in 1981, they expelled him and W-P from their bargaining team because of his unorthodox approach. An arrogant Carney's response was that it was "the best favor they ever did me."

In later years, they would emulate his plans. In fact, it would make an interesting study to see just how much Carney's ideas were emulated and abused by CEOs in the 1990s. Carney would say the following to the *Pittsburgh Times* later:

*One of the last of the typical neighborhood grocery stores in Monessen, this grocery was closed during the development of Westgate when its building was torn down. Note the scales, the wonderful old cash register barely visible on the right, and the product brands on the shelves. (Monessen Redevelopment Authority.)*

*Wheeling-Pittsburgh Steel issued these preferred stocks to its workers in lieu of salary increases and benefits in 1988. Ultimately, they were cashable at pennies on the dollar. (David J. Dyky.)*

> When I first made a preferred stock offering to the employees in 1978, my New York investment bankers said I was crazy—that I'd never be successful. They said the most I'd be able to sell to the employees was $2 million. When 70% of the employees bought $8 million worth, they were shocked.

Monessen was finally beginning to trust the boss's word.

Federal politicians were also opposed to Carney's schemes and W-P was debated in the halls of Congress. Then, along with Senator John Heinz and Congressman Joseph Gaydos, Carney went to Washington. By the time the southwestern Pennsylvania men were done, they had a commitment from the Carter administration to deal with foreign imports, plus a complicated agreement from the Department of Commerce's Economic Development Administration (EDA) and the Farmers Home Loan Administration for all but 10 percent of a $150-million loan. Monessen would have its rail mill and more coke ovens as well.

It was a great day for the city and Carney and yet another innovative plan. In his *Pittsburgh Times* interview, Carney would say, "I knew going in that getting the government loan guarantee would be a tough battle, and it took two years in Washington to get it. Some congressmen fired the bullets, and the other steel companies gave them the ammunition. Most of the big companies don't want to see the small guys modernizing. I won." In 1983, Carney was the winner of the Enterprise Award of the Pittsburgh *Business Times,* an award given to Pittsburgh-area companies who believe in the vision of the entrepreneur and in the building of a fine company through hard work, team spirit, and the desire to contribute to the improvement of the community.

Monessen was leading the way into a brave new world, a world where a lot of people did not want to go. It was an incredible gamble and if it worked, it would change the labor-management-government mix forever. Carney took on the Japanese. He was planning to beat them at their own game by importing Japanese technology. Even the rail mill was Japanese. Next, Monessen received a continuous caster, also Japanese, which was very ambitious for "little steel."

The battle for W-P was on. The workers were getting fed up with always giving out all they had. Their union had negotiated a new contract that helped W-P save itself. In 1983, they took yet another cut to well below what other workers were getting paid. They had families to feed and mortgages to pay. They were the sons and grandsons of the 1919 strikers and they were about to show their meddle. They felt betrayed by everyone.

In the pivotal year of 1985, the view of the steel industry was grim. Without the aid of government, which the Reagan administration refused to give, it was going to be touch and go. W-P had lost so much money that in April of 1985, they filed for bankruptcy. The union contract was up in 1986. The men, in an almost unheard of maneuver, went on strike against a bankrupt company on July 21, 1985. For 98 days, they marched and protested on the streets of Monessen. Were there outside agitators like the strike of 1919? There were certainly outside forces that felt they needed to end Carney's control of W-P. They convinced insiders, like Paul Rusen, the director of District 23 of the Ohio Valley and a Wheeling man, that Carney was the problem. Rusen was more than happy to pass this message on to the men. The workers were more than happy to find someone to blame for all the pain. It was a double-cross, a very costly double-cross for Monessen, who before it was all over, would be double-crossed again.

The men marched. They carried signs. They got into a few pitch battles. They put the blame directly on Dennis Carney. "Carney Must Go!" and "Dennis the Menace" read the signs they carried. And he did go. After negotiating W-P Steel through the most difficult period of its turbulent history, after setting the industry on its ears with innovation after innovation, after fighting the government and Japanese imports, Dennis Carney was blamed for all the troubles and he left. One thing is sure: that was the end of the steel industry in Monessen. The agony would stretch out for several more years, but W-P was finished. Carney, the Mon Valley boy, was the only one trying to keep Monessen alive.

Allen E. Paulson became the new chairman of W-P and new negotiations began. An agreement was reached and the strike ended on October 26. Amid the wage ($21.40 down to $18) and benefit slashing came a new management-labor cooperative agreement similar to Carney's style. The union would get a seat on the board and have a voice in planning. It was yet another precedent-setting innovation that would be copied by major steel companies in their negotiations. That seat was given to Paul Rusen.

Some folks in Monessen were apoplectic, saying this decision violated the original agreement that no one involved with the negotiations would sit on the board. Further than that, it gave the power to Wheeling. Was this Rusen's reward for getting rid of Carney? Mitch Steen, respected historian, newspaper editor, and writer, thought so. He saw the writing on the wall. In an article in the *Tribune-Review,* he quoted Rusen as saying, "I want this corporate headquarters in Wheeling as quick as can be."

The agreement was made in October and Monessen began to unravel the following January. Surely this plan was in the works for some time. How could one of the most modern mills in the world be closed? Monessen had all the ingredients of a profitable mill: a world-class coke plant, a continuous caster, a basic oxygen furnace, and a blast furnace. It didn't matter. In January, the rolling mills and sinter plant in Monessen were permanently closed. In June of 1986, Monessen was on temporary shut down. The blast furnace (Jane) was closed permanently on June 28. The BOF was to be closed permanently on September 2. The men and their families lost all hope.

One man lamented the loss to the *Greensburg Tribune-Review.* "We give concessions. We give money. Now, they don't want no more money, they want bones. I don't believe they are saving the mill. I've been hearing close since 1979. It's like Chinese torture. It's disgusting."

"It [plant] will never open," said Ernie Reppert, the union president in Monessen. One railroader voiced his grief: "I've got 16 years in the mill. I committed myself to this town. I bought a home here. Raised my family here. I'm going to be 46 years old in December. Where do I go?"

Suddenly, three almost surreal things happened. In a shocking maneuver that left the office workers with their mouths open one Friday in August, the Pittsburgh-based main offices of W-P were shut and moved to Wheeling. Paul Rusen was accused as being the mastermind of this maneuver by Mitch Steen in the *Tribune Review* on January 11, 1987. Ray Johnson, a Monessen man working as the public relations officer, asked about the Monessen files. He was told to throw them away. He loaded his car with as much info as he could and headed home to Monessen.

In October, Local 1229 put their building up for sale. At $1,600 a month, it was too expensive to maintain. Originally, the Palace Roller Garden, a skating rink that had opened in the fall of 1919, had been purchased by the union in 1947 in better times. The town had enjoyed bingo, bowling, Christmas parties, and occasional dances. The guts of steel and labor relations were discussed and voted on year after year. Now, the building would be vacant and possibly demolished.

As if in a final thumbing of the nose, the movie *Robocop* began filming in blast furnace alley. They were treading on sacred ground. Men had died here. Men had sweat their life's blood to make iron for steel that would build the country.

144

*In the 1900s, men working near the blast furnace wore 7-pound wooden safety shoes and wrapped their legs in water-drenched burlap bags. In the 1950s, as in this photograph, these workers wore a protective heat veil, an asbestos coat, chrome-leather leggings, and protective gloves. Today, they sit in comfort and press buttons. (Greater Monessen Historical Society.)*

Workers were angry that their mill had come to this. For a donation of $10,000 to the Monessen unemployment committee to buy food for laid-off workers, cops and robbers chased one another where hot iron used to burp, gurgle, and spout red flames in the night sky. Ernie Reppert quit the same month. He had seen the union through the toughest years from 1977. He had had enough.

The rail mill was shut down for good in March of 1987. There was a glut on the market. Carney's vision of rebuilding the infrastructure of the United States did not materialize. The country was letting its infrastructure rot. (Some believe that if a bar mill were erected instead of a rail mill, an arc furnace replaced the BOF, the caster produced bloom and slabs, and the union agreed to combinations of works, the mill would still be working and 800 men would be employed.) The Economic Development Administration (EDA) took over the rail mill to cover its lien and put it up for sale.

The Mon Valley Progress Council, who had helped broker the original deal for the rail mill, helped organize a group of local businessmen to buy the rail mill under the name of the Monongahela Valley Metals Retention and Reuse Committee. They were not the only bidders. Bethlehem Steel, the only competitor for rails in the United States, was also bidding. Bethlehem's intentions were clear. They intended to close the plant permanently. On December 30, 1988, the EDA accepted Bethlehem's bid. The local group tried to buy additional W-P land in Monessen. HABS/HAER tells us, "The group secured financial commitments of nearly one hundred million dollars from federal, state, and private investors for the purchase. The effort fizzled after the sale of the rail mill, however, in part because of uncooperative EDA officials." On the way out the door, W-P paid the Monessen School District $627,938.14 in back taxes and went off to live in Wheeling.

By July of 1987, the international union came calling. They wanted to dissolve the local union. John Cheroki, then Local 1229 president, tried to get a reprieve. It was no use; District 15 was taking over and Monessen's main union was no more. The men responded to the *Valley Independent*:

"We've been raped."

"They really shafted us; they pulled the rug out from under us."

"They're just a bunch of vultures picking over our bones."

"They dumped us as soon as the money ran out, they sold us out for Wheeling."

"I can't believe what they're doing. They're not helping us out at all."

One man wore a black armband to the meeting and shouted, "Got a raw deal all the way down the line."

"Take a look at downtown Monessen. You'll see all the empty storefronts, who will fill them? The city itself will have no income, now that the mill is not operating."

"The local is not out of business. The local is not defunct. We're in a holding pattern until we find out where we're going," said District 15 director Andrew "Lefty" Palm.

Monessen had seen hard times before, but nothing like this. The immigrants had thought they had won a permanent place in America's mainstream when they won their union victory in the 1930s. Who could have anticipated that as the century was drawing to a close, steel was losing its impact in the marketplace and the big mills were too big to handle the new face of the industry? There really was no allegiance. Few could appreciate the continuity years of service had provided. In the end, it would be every man for himself. When new innovations came along, a man had to be ready to change, ready to jump into the breach if he intended to survive and provide for his family. This hard lesson would take Monessen and towns like it throughout southwestern Pennsylvania into a new century to begin picking up the pieces and trying to find a new way of life.

# 10. IS THERE A FUTURE FOR MONESSEN?

As we have seen, Monessen is a typical town in steel country. Her streets look like the streets of Braddock, Duquesne, Rankin, and Homestead. Her ethnic background reflects the same mixture of most steel towns in the Mon Valley. The rich diversity that marked the community throughout its history still exists. The form may be different, but the heritage is celebrated, respected, and honored. The Greek Orthodox Church has bake sales before each holiday, complete with their wonderful pastries. The Slavic and Rusyn communities still carried Easter baskets filled with hams, eggs, and other symbolic ingredients to the church to be blessed. In every ethnic home in Monessen, needlework, loomed cloth, lace tatting, and other handcrafted work are safely tucked away in cedar chests as part of the families' heritage. Men hoard old barrels, old bottles, funnels, and tables where wine and hams were and often are still cured. More than one group make the wonderful *pysanky*, colored eggs decorated in symbolic designs that are given as gifts throughout the year. These traditions are what give Monessen and towns like it up and down the Mon Valley their robust pride and unique heritage. They mark the Mon Valley as irreplaceable for the many different people who came here, learned to live together, and, for nearly 100 years, fought to keep their individual integrity and heritage alive.

Monessen has produced many fine Americans, who have gone on to do good things for themselves, their heritage, and this country. Back in 1918, Sam Moore had a furniture store in Monessen. His aviator son invented the Lazy-Boy chair. In the 1920s, Maude Irwin Owens not only exhibited her painting *Girl with Russian Doll* in the Hall of Negro Artists in New York City, but was also commissioned by the Polish Church in Monessen to do a mural. Hazel Garland became the editor-in-chief of the *New Pittsburgh Courier* in the 1970s. Her daughter Phyllis taught at the Columbia University School of Journalism and was a contributing editor and music editor of *Ebony Magazine*.

Ex-Monessenite Ed Gombos ran for President of the United States in 1996. His most interesting plank was to replace the monetary system with blue money, earned by workers who produce food and goods, and red money, earned by entertainers. "Red money could not be used to buy food and other essentials." This is truly a Monessen attitude. After the IRS gave Gerald Vitale a heap of trouble, he wrote a book called *The Infallibles,* telling people about his company's five-year experience related to its work on Seneca Boulevard in Monessen. Michael Moorer, a Monessen man, won the Boxing Heavyweight Championship of the World when he defeated Evander Holyfield on April 22, 1994. The first left-handed boxer to hold the title, he later lost it to George Foreman. Frances McDormand, who graduated from Monessen in 1975, won an Academy Award for Best Actress in 1996 for her portrayal of a small-town police officer in *Fargo.* All these good folks left Monessen and let their star shine someplace else. One special adult stayed. Albert Lexie, a shoeshine boy, has dedicated his life to helping the kids at Children's Hospital in Pittsburgh. Today, they are known as Albert's Kids and Albert, along with his compassion and tenderness, has been on the *Oprah Winfrey Show.* The list is long. There are more, thousands more, who got their work ethic in this community.

The old "American"-"Foreign"-"Colored" segregation that has lasted for most of the century continues, unfortunately. Ethnicity is no longer the main issue that separates these groups. Too many Monessen folks have intermarried culture to culture. The children of these unions do not have the loyalty to old country rivalries. What hasn't changed, for better or worse, is Republicanism. History has shown that the Republicans do not represent the best interests of the majority of people in Monessen. Monessen needs decent wages for working folks. Republicanism did not offer that in the 1910s, and does not offer it now. The immigrants must be spinning in their graves as they see their hard-won battles being lost once again.

Worse, the immigrants would hang their heads and cry to see that the unions they fought so long and hard to establish have become so powerless in the waning

*The old Pittsburgh Steel buildings were revamped and updated to meet the needs of a new industrial park. Where once 1,000 men worked, now less than 200 do. Where once 90 percent of the workers lived in the Mon Valley, now few do.*

148

years of the twentieth century. The rise to glory was long and hard, but it appears to lack staying power. American unionism in the modern age reached its peak of power in the 1950s when the truckers of the Teamster's Union, in an arrogant abuse of power, shut down the entire country coast-to-coast over a labor dispute. Unions were but 20 years old then, and by the 1970s, when they were about 40 years old, they began to unravel. In all the time that the working man labored for someone else with no one to speak out for him, his voice was heard for less that 50 years before it slipped back into silence. Freedom is eternally gossamer. It tatters easily. What was hard-won by the immigrants when they lifted the common man out of the millenniums of bondage had to be fought for again on the battlefields of Europe in World War II by their sons. Now, after their grandsons endured the loss of the American Dream at the end of the twentieth century, their great-grandchildren must rise up from the opium of drugs, sex, crime, guns, and selfishness that is destroying this country from within to take up the task fought for so long by so many. The future of Monessen will witness these changes.

The road to recovery could not begin until the final humiliations took place. The fallout from the events of the 1980s was enormous. Sharon Steel, although in bankruptcy, bought the coke works and the continuous caster in 1988. They intended to operated the coke ovens under the name of Monessen, Inc., but the EPA said they could not until they fixed the bleeding. They kept the ovens banked. There was one abortive attempt to start up the coke works in 1988, but the EPA shut them down again. Finally, it reopened as Monessen, Inc. in 1989 and 200 men went to work. It was the only industrial site in Monessen that was up and running.

Cannibalizing had been going on for some time. When the open hearth was replaced by the BOF, its giant furnaces were taken out and sent someplace else. When the continuous caster replaced the Blooming Mill, the pits and ingots were shipped elsewhere. In the middle of the night, trucks loaded with mill goodies would drive down Donner or Schoonmaker Avenues headed for the interstates. Like thieves in the night, they were cannibalizing Monessen. By 1991, the tube mill in Allenport, which produced pipe for oil rigs and casing for World War II's big ammunition shells, came tumbling down. The hot strip mill closed and was sold to Casey Equipment Company. Casey Equipment tore down the outside and sold the machinery to a company in the Philippines. In 1992, Bethlehem Steel put the rail mill up for sale. The next year, Bethlehem announced that it would renovate its own aging rail mill in Steelton at the cost of $80 million. By December, Sharon Steel filed for bankruptcy again.

Monessen was nearly bankrupt, especially since it lacked the necessary resources to deal with what was happening on its waterfront and could not find the way to recovery. In 1993, the city and county, with a legislative initiative grant from the state, commissioned a study of the riverfront to determine what to do with the unused but cluttered 2.7 miles of prime land. Over a 26-month period, the riverfront was measured, probed, walked, photographed, and assessed. In the end, it was determined that although there were some environmental issues around the blooming mill and soaking pits of Pittsburgh Steel, on the whole,

149

the land was very exploitable. By 1993, the feasibility study was finished. Some of the Pittsburgh Steel buildings around the Charleroi-Monessen Bridge would be rehabilitated, railroad crossings were to be rehabilitated, and some buildings would be demolished.

In 1994, the Westmoreland County Industrial Development Corporation purchased 25 acres of land from Bethlehem, including all sites from the Charleroi-Monessen Bridge to, but excluding, the rail mill. They purchased additional acreage from Sharon Steel. In the end, they had almost all of the Pittsburgh Steel property except the rail mill and the coke ovens.

Monessen's role in what would happen to its collapsed industrial sites has become catastrophic for the community. Monessen could suggest ideas, but the county authority, without one Monessenite, would have the final decision. With a $5.5-million grant from the state, the work commenced and demolition began. First to come down were the large fabric buildings where men once went deaf making nails. One of the funniest parts of an otherwise sad event was the demolition of the BOF building in June 1995. The interior was long gone, but the building would not come down. They tried on June 1 and June 8, until the structure finally collapsed with a great roar and a huge cloud of black pollution.

In 1991, the Catholic community in Monessen suffered one more devastating blow: the diocese ordered the Catholic churches of Monessen to become one congregation, worshiping together in a single church. It was an ethnic catastrophe as big as the closing of any steel mill and it sent Monessen into a tailspin. It was hard enough to maintain the ethnic roots and traditions of which the community was so proud; now the Catholics were being asked to give them up by the very religion that helped to create them. Monessen rebelled.

However, there were logical reasons why things had to change. The population had decreased and the young people were gone. The older people were hard-pressed to maintain so many churches. That did not make the change any easier. Part of the conflict was that the congregations had sacrificed to build these churches. Incredibly, the Catholics were to discover that the buildings they had built with their money, sacrifices, and initiative did not belong to them. They had no right to them or to anything in them. The baptismal fonts, the Stations of the Cross, the organs, and the smallest pieces of paper belonged to Rome. For a people who had been going through home foreclosures and the loss of jobs, this was not a compassionate, popular dictate. More than the physical building, it was the traditions that the people were fearful of losing. They still wanted to sing Polish, Italian, or Slavic hymns at Christmas. They still wanted to sell their own foods and enjoy their own dances at church events, separate from the other cultures.

By the mid-1990s, new ideas and approaches were stirring, including tourism. The state of Pennsylvania, in a brilliant maneuver, established a number of heritage parks to celebrate the state's diverse industries in oil, lumber, coal, and steel. The Steel Industrial Heritage Association was developed in Homestead to organize a plan to link all the steel towns in a five-county area into a tourism venture. Over the next few years, it created five heritage sites along the Monongahela,

Youghiogheny, and Allegheny Rivers: Homestead for Steel, Connellsville for Coke and Coal, New Kensington for Aluminum, Aliquippa for Steel, and Brownsville for Transportation and Coal. The Heritage Coalition, a newly formed Monessen organization, hooked its dreams for Monessen to this plan hoping to create yet a sixth destination based on little steel and ethnicity. In June of 1995, they collected 3,000 signatures to save a blast furnace and a small bit of acreage for a heritage park with a marina, ethnic restaurants, specialty shops, and heritage events. It was an ambitious plan.

Complicating their efforts were the uncontrollable events occurring on the riverfront. The blast furnaces fell, then the outside shells of the open hearth and blooming mills, and finally, the majestic Pittsburgh Steel office building, an ideal structure for a museum, was demolished. Monessen leadership was skeptical that tourism was viable in the Mon Valley. Few believed that Monessen had anything to offer visitors or that people would be interested in seeing steel mills and eating ravioli, gnocchi, and *perohi*.

The Southwestern Pennsylvania Heritage Preservation Commission, yet another organization dedicated to tourism for Pennsylvania industry, had a study done to see the impact of visitors to the area. The study, done by a Pennsylvania State University economist, found that 500,000 people visited nine Path of Progress

*A HABS/HAER intern looks over Jane Furnace before its demise. The team from the National Park Service was in Monessen for three months, surveying and drawing the blast furnaces and open hearth to record a permanent historical record and place it in the Library of Congress. (Cassandra Vivian.)*

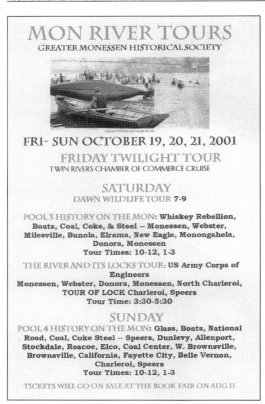

*The Greater Monessen Historical Society sponsors arts programs and book fairs that celebrate local talent, and river cruises that speak of the history of the river and its towns. They are contributing to the revival of Monessen and the Mon Valley. (Greater Monessen Historical Society.)*

sites along various historic highways (U.S. 40 and U.S. 30) in southwestern Pennsylvania in 1993. Their visits impacted the economy by adding $45 million to the communities along the routes, which in turn created nearly 1,000 jobs. Monessen residents received neither a dime, nor a job. Monessen had nothing to draw the visitors to its streets. In 1993, tourism was the third largest retail segment in the United States and the second largest industry in the state of Pennsylvania. Tourism generated over $16.2 billion in revenue in 1990 for the state. By 2005, the projection is that tourism in southwestern Pennsylvania will increase by 30 percent and jobs created by tourism will increase 40 to 50 percent.

Steel Heritage, now called Rivers of Steel Heritage Park, had this to say:

> Rivers of Steel has secured $3.2 million so far, for 11 [river] landings from Kittanning to Brownsville. A landing has been completed at Kittanning on the Allegheny River; construction is pending on the North Shore landing in Pittsburgh. Sites at Arnold (Allegheny) and Brownsville, Charleroi and Monessen (all Monongahela) are in preliminary planning and/or design stages. Plans are underway for four other Monongahela locations, at the Waterfront in Homestead, and Belle Vernon, Monongahela and Donora.

Is Monessen preparing for this venture?

Today, the site of the Homestead mills has done, on a grand scale, exactly what the Heritage Coalition envisioned eight years ago on a smaller scale for Monessen. It has shops, high-end restaurants, and town houses along its riverfront. It is a bustling tourist destination. Pittsburgh's south side, where the mighty J&L mill stood, has diversified into dozens of businesses and new apartment complexes. In each of the five designated heritage sites, progress had been made. Rivers of Steel runs a boat tour of river towns from Pittsburgh to Homestead from spring to fall. Throughout the year, Homestead has a biweekly walking tour of the community for visitors. Braddock, devastated beyond recognition, does the same. These towns have attracted the interest of Elderhostle and have become a part of their program. Brownsville's wharf is complete and plans are underway for tourism on a grand scale with the Flatiron Museum and an upcoming Steamboat Museum. With or without Monessen, these projects have happened.

In recent years, Monessen has begun to move, too. The Heritage Coalition has changed its name to the Greater Monessen Historical Society. It has accomplished an amazing amount of work leading to the early vision of the Heritage Coalition. Under the guidance of the Pennsylvania Council for the Arts and the Pennsylvania Humanities Council, a short play has been written called *Titanic: The Monessen Story*. An annual local author and publisher book fair is held each year to celebrate local writers and themes. Like in Homestead, a Mon River cruise featuring historic narration, was inaugurated last year. Folks within a 50-mile radius came to town. People visited from as far as Texas. A class in urban history at California University of Pennsylvania used Monessen artifacts and collected Monessen oral histories to instill pride in local communities and teach students how to value and interpret local history.

In 1994, under a grant from the Southwestern Pennsylvania Heritage Preservation Commission, another organization, Vintage of Pittsburgh, did a series of programs in valley towns called "Voices of Italian Americans in Southwestern Pennsylvania." They held six meetings with six topics based on restoring and preserving ethnic traditions. The Monessen group decided to continue to study its roots and heritage by founding an organization dedicated to recording and preserving Italian heritage. Today, over 200 strong, they hold monthly meetings and have speakers usually related to Italian themes. Little emphasis is placed on recording and preserving heritage, which was the original intent of the organization, but the sheer numbers show the hunger descendents of immigrants have to rediscover their roots.

Another group, of international scope, is the Carpatho-Rusyn Society, whose founder and president John Righetti was born and bred in Monessen of an Italian-American father and a Carpatho-Rusyn-American mother. The group owes its origin to the Monessen Cultural Heritage Festival. When the festival encouraged Monessenites to participate with food, dance, and crafts, Saint John's Russian Orthodox Church, along with several other churches, responded by encouraging their young people to get involved. The Carpathian Youth Choir and Dancers was formed. Righetti tells us it was "only the second Carpatho-Rusyn performing ensemble founded in America since the 1950s." Out of this effort, Righetti became inspired and he is now a leader in the Rusyn-American community nationwide. He has served on the board of the Carpatho-Rusyn Research Center, which is the country's best organization for studying the people and their culture. He represented the community at the International World Congress of Rusyns in Krynica, Poland in 1993. He founded the Carpatho-Rusyn Society in 1994. Today, it has seven United States chapters and promotes Carpatho-Rusyn culture "on both sides of the Atlantic."

However, tourism and history are just a few ways in which Monessen is approaching recovery. The Douglas School of Business, now the Douglas Education Center, has been around for a long time as a business school teaching skills like computers and taking a backseat to the mills. In recent years, it has come to the forefront in Monessen as an up-and-coming school in southwestern Pennsylvania; perhaps Lou Manderino's dream for Monessen back in the 1960s is coming true. Its biggest venture is in the realm of motion picture artistry, as in make-up special effects. With the acquisition of nationally known make-up artist Tom Savini as an instructor, young people from around the world are flocking to the worn-out town to learn a trade. Douglas's visionary leader Jeffrey D. Imbrescia has recently added a second program that will increase the school's profile and bring more young, talented people to the community. Douglas is instituting a 16-week cinema animation program. The students these projects will draw need housing, places to eat, and places to play. They need stores to buy supplies. They need some intellectual stimulation. There are dozens of buildings surrounding the Douglas Campus awaiting the artist, the sculptor, the entrepreneur, and the coffeeshop owner to join the revival.

In 1980, Matthew S. Magda's *Monessen: Industrial Boomtown and Steel Community 1898–1980* was published. Magda ended his book by asking a few citizens for their predictions for the future of Monessen. Most, like R. Mitch Steen, Christina Kerekes, and John Czelen, thought the rail mill would keep Monessen alive. Stephen Wisyanski, a longtime international union representative from Monessen, who died in 2001, offered little hope for the future. Joseph Barton thought Monessen would turn into a place for senior citizens. As Monessen enters a new millennium and century, we can make a few more predictions.

Susanna Swade left Monessen after college, lived abroad for a number of years in Japan and Germany, then settled in Columbus, Ohio where she became the principal of an elementary school. After she retired, she came home to Monessen where she volunteers for Meals on Wheels, the Literacy Council, and various other community projects. She predicts the following:

> I would like to see Monessen become the cultural hub of the mid-Mon Valley. This could be accomplished in several ways. First, the present Monessen Public Library and District Center could be expanded to include an auditorium where plays, theatrical events, musicals, and

lectures could be held. Then, the addition of such businesses as a multi-plex movie theater, art galleries, book stores, coffee shops, and ethnic restaurants could become a part of the downtown areas. The centerpiece of our cultural hub would be the History Museum developed by the Greater Monessen Historical Society. The museum would contain exhibits relating to the ethnic and industrial heritage of Monessen and the Mon Valley. Tourism could also be brought to the region with boat tours on the Monongahela River and walking tours throughout our town relating the rich history of this diverse community.

Jack Bergstein never left. He went to school at Penn State and law school at Duquesne University. For awhile, he was an elected member of city council and still plays a role in public life in Monessen. Jack believes that Monessen will survive:

> Monessen can come back. It will require cooperation by local, state, and Federal officials. It will require contributions by the citizens. Most importantly it will require leadership with vision. I see a larger metropolitan community such as the Greater Mon Valley with new highways, new developments like Southpointe, and the sharing of resources among the various valley communities. With a little luck Monessen will continue to be a viable place to live.

*The Carpathian Youth Choir and Dancers of Monessen were founded by John Righetti. The formation of this group led to the creation of the Carpatho-Rusyn Society of the 1990s. (Carpatho Rusyn Society.)*

Ed Mikula Sr. is more specific. Mikula lived in Monessen all his life, married, and raised five children. He worked as a draftsman in the engineering department of Pittsburgh Steel and experienced the shut-down of the industry first hand. He has faith in the city:

> Can Monessen once again have the vibrancy of past years? Can ascendency be in our future? The resounding answer is: of course! That hope rests in the future development of the Mon River Waterfront. The development must include, among other things, a marina, first run movie theatre, and the very important foot traffic: a carosel, playgrounds, kids sprinkler, parklets, green spaces, ethnic eateries, ice cream shop and a coffee shop. All this with a view of the beautiful Monongahela River. What will it take to accomplish this ascendancy? Hard work, always a trait of Monessenites, vision, and of course money! Money from both private and government funds. Can the city of Monessen move to ascendancy? I think it can in a cooperative effort. Somehow! Someway! Someday!

Monessen needs an infusion of the immigrant spirit that created the town. It is looking for a few good people. It has empty homes, some of them eligible for National Register status, that the town will practically give away to people who will repair them. Some of these homes are the once elegant mansions along Silk Stocking Row. The city boasts a Rehab for Resale program, administered through the Mon Valley Initiative, where families may purchase and renovate homes for very reasonable rates. The Mon Valley Initiative wants to fill the community with good families with young children. The Monessen schools have a 13 to 1 teacher-pupil ratio and send more than 78 percent of their graduates on to technical schools and colleges. Some people believe that the schools' biggest asset is not merging with other districts. Monessen schools have Monessen kids and that means Monessen pluses and minuses.

The riverfront is in the hands of the county, unfortunately, and county officials do not seem to care very much what Monessen wants. Downtown Monessen has empty historic buildings, which could present an opportunity of a lifetime to anyone tired of commuting to work in the rat race. One can live upstairs and do business downstairs, an old system that is being revived in new upscale communities. Lucchesi's Restaurant in Monessen is a perfect example of good business surviving in a small town. This high-end, privately owned establishment thrives, against all odds, in an old beer garden and brings upscale folks from the tri-state area to town each and every evening. The restaurant not only survived the demolition of the community, but it is the shining example of how the community can succeed. There are people who want to come back. Those who are here must give them something to come back to.

Go Greyhounds!

# BIBLIOGRAPHY

Bjorkfors, Peter. *The Finns on the Titanic.* www.utu.fi/erill/instmigr/art/titanic.html.

Boucher, John Newton. *Old and New Westmoreland.* Vol. 1, 2, 3, 4. New York: The American Historical Society, 1918.

Brody, David. *Labor in Crisis: The Steel Strike of 1919.* Urbana: University of Illinois Press, 1987.

Butler, Elizabeth Beardsley. *Women and the Trades, Pittsburgh, 1907–1908.* New York: Charities Publication Committee, 1909.

Christ Evangelical Lutheran Church. *History of Our City.* Columbus: Lutheran Book Concern, *c.* 1902–1903.

Collier, Richard. *The Plague of the Spanish Lady: The Influenza Pandemic of 1918–1919.* N.p.: Allison and Busby, 1996.

Davies, Jean and Students of the Monessen Jr. Sr. High School. *Traveling Through Time in Monessen, PA.* Monessen: Mon Valley Education Consortium Great Idea Grant, 1993.

Dickerson, Dennis C. *Out of the Crucible: Black Steelworkers in Western Pennsylvania, 1875–1980.* Albany: State University of New York Press, 1986.

Foster, William Z. *The Steel Strike of 1919: A Sample of Primary Sources.* Chicago Metro History Center. http://www.uic.edu/orgs/cmhec/steel.html.

——. *The Great Steel Strike And Its Lessons.* New York: B.W. Huebsch, Inc., 1920.

Garbarino, William. *Along the Monongahela: A History of Early Events Along the Monongahela and its Tributaries.* N.p.: Midway Publishing, 2000.

Hoerr, John P. *And The Wolf Finally Came: The Decline of the American Steel Industry.* Pittsburgh: University of Pittsburgh Press, 1988.

Interchurch World Movement of North America. *Report on the Steel Strike of 1919 by the Commission of Inquiry, the Interchurch World Movement, Bishop Francis J. McConnell, chairman.* New York: Harcourt, Brace and Company, 1920.

Interchurch World Movement of North America. *Public Opinion and the Steel Strike; supplementary reports of the investigators to the Commission of Inquiry, the Interchurch World Movement, Bishop Francis J McConnell, chairman.* New York: Harcourt, Brace and Company, 1921.

Jenkins, Philip. *Hoods and Shirts: The Extreme Right in Pennsylvania, 1925–1950.* Chapel Hill: University of North Carolina Press, 1997.

Kolehmainen, John I. *A History of the Finns in Ohio, Western Pennsylvania and West Virginia*. N.p.: Ohio Finnish-American Historical Society, 1937.

Loucks, Emerson H. *The Ku Klux Klan in Pennsylvania*. New York-Harrisburg: The Telegraph Press, 1936.

Magda, Matthew S. *Monessen: Industrial Boomtown and Steel Community 1898–1980*. Harrisburg: Pennsylvania Historical and Museum Commission, 1985.

*McCabe Family Papers*. Archives of Industrial Society. University of Pittsburgh Libraries, Scrapbooks, Box 6. Summary: Correspondence and business papers of H. Dallas McCabe (1872–1925).

McCormick, Charles H. *Seeing Reds: Federal Surveillance of Radicals in the Pittsburgh Mill District, 1917–1921*. Pittsburgh: University of Pittsburgh Press, 1997.

*Monessen's Celebration of its Twenty-Fifth Anniversary*. Monessen Board of Trade, 1923.

Monessen Centennial Booklet. Monessen, PA, 1998.

Monessen City Directory. Polk's Monessen County Directory 1924–1925.

Monessen Diamond Jubilee Booklet. Monessen, PA, 1973.

Monessen Golden Jubilee Booklet. Monessen, PA, 1948.

Murray, Robert K. *Red Scare: A Study In National Hysteria, 1919–1920*. N.p.: University of Minnesota Press, 1955.

Nummi, Gerald E. and Janet A. White. *I'm Going to See What Has Happened: The Personal Experience of 3rd Class Finnish Titanic Survivor, Mrs. Elin Hakkarainen*. N.p.: J.A. White, 1996.

Olds, Marshall. *Analysis of the Interchurch World Movement Report on the Steel Strike*. New York: GP Putnam's Sons, 1922.

Parker, Arthur. *The Monongahela: River of Dreams, River of Sweat*. University Park: Pennsylvania State University Press, 1999.

Russell, Stephen V. *Mid Mon Valley All Sports Hall of Fame Biographical Journal*. Roscoe: Mid Mon Valley All Sports Hall of Fame, 2002.

Schendel, Gordon. "Something Is Rotten in the State of Pennsylvania." *Collier's Magazine*. 11 November 1950: 18, 19, 64–70.

Sinchak, Michael. *Slovenské spevy a tance / upravil a vlastny'm nákladom vydal: Michal Sincak. Hudbu na piano slozil: Samuel Sinchak. Slovak songs and dances, arranged and published by Michael Sinchak*. Music and piano arrangement by Samuel Sinchak. Monessen, PA, *c*. 1942.

Sweet, Beryle G. *A Brief History of Page Fence*. http://www.telerama.com/~cass/Pagefence.html.

Vivian, Cassandra and Michael Workman. Interview of Union Presidents of Local 1229. Monessen: Greater Monessen Historical Society, July 11, 1995.

Weston, Bruce. *Monessen: Story of a Steel Town. Southwestern Pennsylvania*. N.p.: Museum of Southwestern Pennsylvania, 1983.

Workman, Michael E., with assistance by Cassandra Vivian. *A History of Pittsburgh Steel Company's Monessen Works*. HAER, National Park Service, April 1996.

Wright, Richard. *The Negro in Pennsylvania: A Study in Economic History*. New York: 1969.

# INDEX

28th Division, 99, 101–102

Adams, Avery, 107, 122

AFL CIO, 98, 120, 126, 133

Amalgamated Association of Iron, Steel, and Tin Workers, 50–51, 56

American Chain Co., 19, 62

American Steel Hoops Co., 18–19

American Tin Plate Co., American Sheet and Tin Plate Co., 17, 40

Ames, Fred, 45

Arch Tavern, 34, 110–111, 116, 129

Army-Navy E Award, 99

Beery, J. Karl, 98, 104

Bergstein, Jack, 155

Bouquet Flats, 35, 96–97

Bumbaugh, W.S., 17

Calderone, Tony and Rose, 111

Carney, Dennis J., 140–145

Carpatho Rusyn, 25, 28, 61, 153–155

Civil Works Administration, 85

Collier's Magazine, 116–118

Cultural Heritage Festival, 136–137, 153

D'Alessio, Dr. Joseph, 96, 108–110

Donner, William H., 14

Douglas Education Center, 152

Dutchtown, 25, 64

East Side Land Co., 13, 15–16, 21, 34, 44

Eastgate Urban Renewal Project, 27, 125–126, 128–129

Essen Land Co., 15

Ferencz, Michael, 108

Finnish Socialist Hall, 34

Finnish Temperance Hall, 34, 70

Firemen's Band, 71, 72

Fordham, 13

Gary, Judge Elbert, 53, 58–60

Getodo Club, 113–114, 117, 119–121, 137

Gibson, Josh, 86

Gibsonton Distillery, 12, 48, 49

Greater Monessen Historical Society, 127, 153, 155

HABS/HAER, 125, 145, 151

Hamilton Co., 13

Henrich, Tom, 86

Heritage Coalition, 151, 153

Howes, Reverend Allan J., 117–121

Industrial Baseball League, 86

Johnson's Restaurant, 23, 97, 99, 116, 132, 138, 139

Keystone Magazine, 30, 35, 94, 100

Lescanac, Joseph, 41, 95, 103–104

Liberty Bond, 42, 58, 70

Liberty Loan Drive, 43, 44

Longo, Tony, 114–115

Louhi Band, 34, 70–71, 76

Love, Ruth, 118–119

Manderino, James (Jim, Jimmy), 101, 124

Manderino, Lou (Louis), 124, 128, 135–136, 154

Manos Theater, 41, 87, 93, 97, 137

Manown, William J., 13, 15

Maxwell, Allison R. Jr., 122, 140

Mayo, John, 91

McCabe, H. Dallas, 15, 17, 46, 75

McMahon family, 11, 13, 15–16
McShaffrey, William A., 20, 70, 131
Mid–Atlantic League Class D Baseball, 84
Mikula, Ed, 156
Minnie, Ron, Ronald, 129–130
Mon Valley Initiative, 156
Monessen
    Municipal Airport, 80–81, 88, 110
    Board of Trade, 20, 50
    Brewery, 11, 18, 40, 48, 94, 96
    Cardinals, 84
    Distilling Company, 12, 21
    Drum Corp, 71–72
    Fife and Drum Corps, 71
    Foundry and Machine Co, 15, 17–18,
        62–63, 94, 97, 99, 109
    Greyhounds, 132
    News, 16, 21, 47, 93–94, 102, 104
    Park Plan, 9, 93, 96, 106, 126
    Public Library & Dist. Center, 114, 154
*Monessen Daily Independent*, The, 37, 122
Monongahela River, 9–12, 48, 66, 122, 134,
    155–156
Ninth Street Park, 85, 87
NIPA (North Italian Political Assoc.), 32,
    72, 89
Nicksich, George, 131
Olsavick family, 27, 68
Operation Crusade, 109, 118–119, 135
P&LE, 14, 17, 59, 89, 96, 106, 114–115, 131
Page Park, 66, 72, 85–86
*Page Patter*, 94
Page Steel & Wire Co., 81, 86, 88, 92–94,
    97, 99, 123, 140
Page Woven Wire & Fence Co., 18–19, 27,
    57, 60–62
Parente, Hugo J., 103–105, 108–112, 118,
    121, 127–129, 135–136
Park Casino, 110–111, 133
Program of Progress, 107, 140, 151–152
Pittsburgh Freight Zone, 12
Pittsburgh Steel Coal & Iron Police, 45, 55
Pittsburgh Steel Co., 17–21, 24, 26–27,
    30–31, 35–36, 39–42, 46, 49–51, 53,

57–58, 60–61, 71, 77, 79–80, 82, 86,
    89–90, 93–94, 97, 99, 100–101, 103,
    106–107, 113–114, 122–125, 129–134,
    138, 142, 148–151, 154
Pittsburgh Steel Products Co., 26, 46, 57,
    71, 80
Polish National Alliance, 27, 87, 91
Program for Profits, 122–123, 140
Red Hanger, 110
Redevelopment Authority, 124–125
Righetti, John, 29, 154–155
Rowe, Wallace J., 19
Rusen, Paul, 143–144
Schoonmaker, James M., 13
Schuck, C.L., 21, 94–96, 98, 117
Seneca Heights, 127
Sheetz Hotel, 25, 48
Silk Stocking Row, 23, 26, 82, 135, 156
Sinchak, Michael, 73–74
Sinchak, Stephen, 96, 108
Spielman, John, 105
Standard Land and Improvement Co., 15
Star Theater, 22–23, 97, 106, 131, 138
SWOC (Steel Workers Organizing
    Committee), 91–92, 98
Steen, Mitch, 18, 144, 154
Strike of 1919, 26, 36, 40, 50, 90, 143
Swade, Susanna, 154
*Valley Independent*, 21, 122, 124, 135, 140, 146
Tin Mill, 14, 17, 27, 30, 33–34, 37, 40,
    56–57, 75, 80–81
*Titanic*, 36–39, 153
Twin Coaches, 73, 111–112
UROBYA (United Russian Orthodox
    Brotherhood of America), 29
Victoria, David, 96
Westgate, 26, 122, 125–126, 128, 141
Westmoreland County, 9, 17, 21, 41, 47–48,
    50, 67, 85, 95–96, 109, 114, 117, 119, 135,
    150
Wheeling-Pittsburgh Steel, 134, 138,
    140–146
Wireton, 26, 42, 57, 62
Youghiogheny, 11, 151